Lewis Campbell

Some Aspects of the Christian Ideal

Lewis Campbell

Some Aspects of the Christian Ideal

ISBN/EAN: 9783337033361

Printed in Europe, USA, Canada, Australia, Japan

Cover: Foto ©Lupo / pixelio.de

More available books at **www.hansebooks.com**

SOME ASPECTS

OF

THE CHRISTIAN IDEAL:

SERMONS

BY THE

REV. L. CAMPBELL, M.A., LL.D.

Professor of Greek in the University of St. Andrews

LONDON

MACMILLAN AND CO.

1877

THIS BOOK IS DEDICATED

TO MY WIFE,

𝔉𝔯𝔞𝔫𝔠𝔢𝔰 𝔓𝔦𝔱𝔱 ℭ𝔞𝔪𝔭𝔟𝔢𝔩𝔩,

WITHOUT WHOSE HELP

NEITHER THIS NOR OTHER EFFORTS

WOULD HAVE BEEN POSSIBLE TO ME.

PREFACE.

THIS volume is not a contribution to theology. It consists of sermons, preached at various times, and under different circumstances, during the last fifteen years. They had for the most part a very simple aim, viz., that combined exhortation and encouragement, which was known among the early Christians as παράκλησις: and I have consented to their publication in the 'trembling hope' that some persons besides those for whom they were first meant, may derive comfort from them in the present time of transition.

I have made no attempt to work these short discourses into a connected whole. They are printed as they were preached, with a few unimportant omissions and the removal of some of the faults of language, which it is to be feared are still too numerous. In a few instances, where for divers reasons it seemed desirable, I have inserted the date of composition.

The reader who is troubled by certain inequalities of style, is requested to bear in mind that the sermons were not originally intended for the same congregation. Some of them belong to the period of the writer's brief ministry in the Church of England, as the Vicar of Milford, in Hampshire; one was written for delivery at a Presbyterian service in a Scottish country school; and the address with which the volume closes was first given at a Sunday-evening meeting in the chief School-room of Clifton College. As to the greater number, which were written at St. Andrews, those who know something of the benign influences existing in the old Cathedral city will readily understand that while some were designed for the Episcopalian congregation there, others were originally preached in the College Church, or in the Town Churches of St. Andrew and St. Mary.

CONTENTS.

ERRATA.

Page   39, line 18, *for* from *read* for.

„   87,   „   11, *for* life *read* the life.

„   269,   „   10, *for* a conscious *read* an unconscious.

SERMON I.

THE DUTY OF OUTSPOKENNESS ON RELIGIOUS QUESTIONS.

1870.

'Seeing then that we have such hope, we use great plainness of speech: and not as Moses, which put a vail over his face, that the children of Israel could not stedfastly look to the end of that which is abolished.'—2 COR. iii. 12, 13.

TRUE Religion is very simple and very deep. As simple as this statement, 'God is good;' as deep as life and death, or anything which we can imagine that is deeper still.

But it has ever been hard for men to receive religion in all its simplicity and in all its depth. They want something they can touch and handle, something to fill the imagination, something with many colours to attract the eye, with various melodies to content the ear, something to move their feelings through their senses. They cannot live in the pure serenity of perfect light; they get tired of the monotonous sound of goodness and mercy, righteousness and truth. They must have a form as well as a substance, a letter as well as a spirit; they

B

receive religion, as St. Paul would say, according to the flesh.

And human teachers have ever been ready to adapt themselves to this craving, and have put their teaching into a shape in which they thought it most likely to be received; so that even when, as in the story of Moses, their own countenance really shone with the light of God, they have put a veil between themselves and the people. And such is the grossness of the mind and apprehension of man that, after a time, the veil comes to be worshipped more than the glory which it partly hides, the earthly vessel is more thought of than the heavenly treasure. Then if some one comes and says to men, This vessel which contains your treasure, this lamp which carries the enlightening oil, is earthly and of the earth, and were it broken, the heavenly fire would only shine more brightly;—if some one tries to draw away the veil;—do you think they will believe him or listen to him? Will they not at once cry out upon him for an irreligious and godless man, who would deprive them of the comfort of their religion?

And yet it is sometimes the part of the Christian minister and teacher, in following the example of Christ and of St. Paul, to 'use great plainness of speech:' to tell the people, not what they most wish or expect to hear, not what is most in accordance

with their previous ideas and prejudices, but what
he himself thinks and knows, what he has found
in his own experience to be of lasting value, or, in
Scriptural language, the truth which he believes that
he has heard of God.

St. Paul made the greatest effort that was ever
made by any one, excepting only Christ, to bring
men to receive a spiritual religion. He strove to
show to the Jew that God in Christ was the Father
of all men, and not of the Jew only; that righteousness meant not the mere outward performance of
certain acts, but a right attitude of the heart towards
God; he strove to make the Gentiles see that
'God who made the world and all things therein,
dwelleth not in temples made with hands, neither
is worshipped with men's hands, as though He needed
anything, seeing He giveth to all life and breath and
all things,' that He hath made of one blood all the
nations of men, and that He hath appointed a day
in which to judge the world in righteousness by
one whom He hath ordained. And we read in this
Epistle to the Corinthians that this teaching of
St. Paul was 'to the Jews a stumblingblock and to
the Greeks foolishness.' Now, why was this?

Let us try to imagine how they must have felt in
listening to him. Let us imagine the Jew being
told that the Law of Moses was abolished and done
away, that the blood of bulls and goats could not

take away sin ; that the Passover, the commemoration of the great deliverance that had first made
the Jews a nation, was only a type and a shadow
which was vanishing ; that the peculiar people must
no longer think that Jehovah had any special
regard for them, but must learn to embrace the
Gentiles, who for half their lives had been polluting
themselves with abominations of idols ? Was this,
the Jewish objector might say, was this, indeed, to
stand upon the ancient paths and to restore the
desolations of many generations ? Was it not rather
to remove the landmarks, to tear up the foundations,
to plough over the ruined city, nay, to desert the
ancient people who were called by the name of Jehovah, and to be joined to the corruptions of those
who were not a people, but were common and un-
clean ? Is it wonderful that this should be a stumblingblock to the Jews ? that those who clung to the
old narrow traditions failed to take in all the new
and larger hope? that they could not suffer the
Hope of Israel to be diluted into the Hope of Man ?
or that he who seemed to rob them of their heart's
treasure was thought by them no better than an
infidel ? Is it wonderful that they called by the
name of heresy that way after which he worshipped
the God of his fathers, or that they cried out, when
he proclaimed his message, 'Away with such a fellow
from the earth, for it is not fit that he should live ?'

Is it not rather wonderful that so many, imperfectly indeed, and with continual danger of relapsing into Judaism, were found to believe the Gospel?

Such then was the nature of the offence which the teaching of St. Paul gave to the Jew. Let us now turn and ask what impression it was likely to produce upon the Gentiles. I think I hear one of them crying, 'What will this babbler say? And are we not to worship the sun going forth as a giant to run his course, nor the moon walking in brightness, nor the earth, great bounteous mother of all things that live, nor the glorious heaven that smiles on us with pure radiance in the daytime and gazes on us with a thousand eyes at night? These are no gods, forsooth, nor may we worship that in which the glory of the world is centred, the beauteous form of man, in action so express and admirable, in thought and reason so like a god—this image glorified by art, and deified to be the token and symbol to us of Nature's infinite powers. The Diana of the Ephesians, the Jupiter of Lystra or of Athens, these are to be nothing to us. Those are no gods, you tell us, that are made with hands. The philosopher may perhaps agree with you so far, but what is to become of the poor and ignorant multitude? Would you take from them their only stay, the only consolation which they have amid the miseries of their feeble life, and offer them instead an unseen God,

to be comprehended only with the mind! Take heed
that you are not destroying what you cannot restore.'
It needed not the sordid interests of the guild of
image-makers, of those of like occupation with Demetrius, including those other craftsmen who dealt
in oracles and sacrifices, to give to these objections
an overwhelming strength. The wonder is not that
St. Paul appeared an atheist to Demetrius as he
had appeared an infidel to Sosthenes, nor that he
seemed to the Athenians to be a setter forth of
strange gods, as if Jesus were one more to be added
to their gods many and lords many, and the Resurrection a sort of goddess, like the goddess of victory.
It is not wonderful that not many mighty, not many
learned, not many noble were called from among the
Gentiles into the early Church. It is rather wonderful that so many should have been found to flock
into it, though the wonder is abated when we
consider the divine strength of Christianity and the
decrepitude of the old religions.

Now St. Paul was not the first nor the last who in
teaching a spiritual religion, in trying to open a way
between the soul of man and the Spirit of God, has
won for himself amongst the people of his own time
the name of a godless and irreligious man.

Even Moses, in warning the Jews against idolatry,
in giving them the name of Jehovah (the Eternal
Being, merciful and gracious, forgiving iniquity, &c.),

in teaching them to respect the stranger and the fatherless, was already seeking to take away some folds of the thick veil which was upon their heart. But with what result? Did they at once believe in an Unseen God, or accept the law of mercy and truth as an essential part of their religion? Did they not, when Moses himself was withdrawn from them for a time into spiritual communion with Jehovah, turn away from their true prophet and lawgiver, and say unto Aaron the priest, 'Make us gods to go before us, for as for this Moses, which brought us out of the land of Egypt, we wot not what is become of him.'

Then many ages afterwards, when the idea or rather the formality of sacrifice had settled down like a mouldy and clammy fur upon the hearts of the people, and the land was notwithstanding defiled with innocent blood, the voice of Isaiah is heard proclaiming in the name of God, 'Your new moons and your appointed feasts my soul hateth, they are a trouble unto me, I am weary to bear them. Bring no more vain oblations. Cease to do evil, learn to do well: seek judgment, relieve the oppressed, judge the fatherless, plead for the widow.'

And Ezekiel is heard to cry, 'The son shall not bear the iniquity of his father. The soul that sinneth, it shall die.' But Isaiah fell a victim to the idolatrous fanaticism of his countrymen, and of

Ezekiel the people said, 'Doth he not speak parables?'
And so all the Hebrew Prophets, one by one, bore
witness equally against the formalism and idolatry of
the people, and were rejected equally, and that in
the name of religion, by the professed worshippers of
Jehovah and of Baalim. So that our Saviour could
say to His own countrymen, 'Ye build the tombs of
the prophets and your fathers killed them,' and to
Jerusalem, 'Thou that killest the prophets and
stonest them that are sent unto thee.' And Stephen
to his accusers, 'Which of the prophets have not
your fathers persecuted?'

And what of Christ Himself? Was He not put to
death for blasphemy: because he had said, 'Destroy
this temple and in three days I will raise it up,' and
because He told the Chief Priests that 'The hour was
coming when the Son of Man should sit on the right
hand of Power?' His enemies affected to believe that
He had actually threatened to destroy the temple.
His disciples after the resurrection understood Him
to have been speaking of the temple of His body.
But the more we dwell on those divine words the
wider seems to be their meaning. For the body of
Christ, as St. Paul says, is the Communion of believers everywhere, and Christ seems to say to us in
these words—Let outward forms and ceremonies
perish, as they will, let institutions and their modes

of government be altered or abolished, let human doctrines shift and decay, still the principle of religion is indestructible in the heart of man, the Kingdom of Heaven within us is Eternal, the Spirit of Worship is there imperishable. Fear not but God will give it a body as it shall please Him. And the fulness of this spirit and of this power is in the mind of Christ, who raises up anew continually the temple that is made without hands.

I will cite one more example from the history of our own country. Have you ever tried to think of what happened in this very city and within this church at the Reformation? Did it ever strike you how the minds of many good and pious persons must have been shocked, when they were told by the Reformers that the sacrifice of the mass was no sacrifice at all, that there was no virtue in priestly absolution, that to confess their sins to a priest was unnecessary, useless, and wrong? How must they have felt when the crucifixes, before which they had worshipped with streaming eyes, were thrown down and broken, when the beautiful shrines and altars, where, as they believed, the body of Christ had been daily offered for their sins, were demolished, and the carved work thereof, in St. Andrews and elsewhere, was broken to pieces with axes and hammers? Is it surprising that the Reformers were called infidels and heretics, or that many persons besides the priests

and monks were incensed at them? Why there are
some good people in England to this day, though I am
glad to say not many, who look upon Scotland as a
sort of heathen country, and why? Not because of
the national vices, or the growth of irreligion in large
towns, not because you have drunkards in your streets,
and innocent lives are perishing without any regarding them — but because you have no altars in your
churches, because your ministers are not ordained by
bishops, and because you think of the Holy Communion only as a joint commemoration of the death
of Christ. Read the letters which are appearing daily
in the newspapers from Roman Catholics about the
Italian occupation of Rome, and you will understand
something of the feeling of those old times. By the
efforts and by the blood of the Reformers, a veil was
taken away from the hearts of this people, and in some
ways we now see more clearly. There is little fear
that the people of Scotland at least will ever again
be led blindfold by any priesthood, or will be again
tempted to exaggerate the mystery of the sacraments.
The great truth of the Eternal Faithfulness of God
as the ground of our faith in Him ('I am the Lord,
I change not, therefore ye sons of Jacob are not
consumed,') which has ever been the corner-stone
of Scottish Theology, has sunk deep down into the
hearts of the people, and only needs to be applied,
both in theory and practice, in order to its shining

forth more brightly than before. And there are many ways in which we seem to have been led almost unconsciously, to throw off some fetters by which our fathers were still held. I will try to make my meaning clearer by an illustration. A few evenings since we were many of us gazing with delight at a beautiful appearance in the heavens. The time has been when such an appearance would have been looked upon with superstitious fear, as if God Himself were holding forth a signal to the world. It would have been supposed to be a direct token and forewarning of evil to come. It would have been said that the heavens, as troubled with man's act, threaten his bloody stage : that the heavens themselves blaze forth the fall of princes[1]. Now is it a loss or a gain to us that we have ceased to regard the matter in this way? Do we the less believe in God, in one who rules amongst the children of men, because we have been taught that there is a world of nature, into which human passions do not enter,

---

[1] *Casca.*   When these prodigies
Do so conjointly meet, let not men say
'These are their causes, they are natural:'
For I believe they are portentous things
Unto the climate that they point upon.
    Cicero. Indeed, it is a strange—disposed time :
But men may construe things after their fashion,
Clean from the purpose of the things themselves.

which goes on its way unruffled and undisturbed by the sinfulness or heroism of mankind? Do we the less believe in a righteous judgment of God, because we see clearly that He judges men and nations through their own actions, and that the lessons of history are to be read apart from the truths of physical science? The warning of the Hebrew preacher still remains as true as the day it was spoken: 'If thou seest oppression and strife in a city, marvel not at the matter, for He that is higher than the highest regardeth, and there be higher than they.'

We need not fear, then, or be discouraged, if it should be found that in some matters either of doctrine or of custom and tradition, there is still a veil upon the people's heart which clouds for them the perfect vision of the righteousness and goodness, the justice and mercy, of Almighty God: nor should the Christian teacher, who thinks he sees it is so, shrink from trying to remove the veil: if he may hope thereby to bring the minds of his countrymen nearer to a pure and spiritual religion. Least of all is he to be deterred by the imputation of impiety, or of infidelity and atheism, which has been shared by all religious teachers who have had anything to tell mankind, including Christ Himself. But there is not time at present to pursue this subject further, and I will therefore conclude with a few practical precepts.

And they shall be as far as possible in the words of Christ.

1. Remember always that the kingdom of heaven is within you. You have many things to help you in becoming better :—the reading of the Bible, the preaching of the gospel, prayers and psalms, the common round of duties, the intercourse of Christian friends, the experience of life. But unless you do become better, the kingdom of heaven is not come to you; it has only come near to you, it has not touched you nor entered in. The kingdom of heaven is not in preaching or hearing, or in Sabbath keeping, or in any outward act, but in righteousness, and peace, and joy in the Holy Spirit of God. And the only outward proof by which you can know that you have the kingdom of God within, and apart from this proof you cannot know it, is, that you are ceasing to do evil, that you are learning to do well.

2. The second precept is—Remember how Christ said, there is no commandment greater than these two, Thou shalt love the Lord thy God with all thy heart, and soul, and strength; and, Thou shalt love thy neighbour as thyself. Remember also, that to love God is to do His will : and what doth the Lord require of thee but to do justly, and to love mercy, and to walk humbly with thy God? And if you ask of Christ, Who is my neighbour? He answers you in the parable of the Good Samaritan; Not he that

is nearest to you in kindred and family, or in being
of the same nation or of the same Church, or body of
Christian men, but he that is nearest to you in this
one way, that you have the power and opportunity
of doing him any good, or of preventing any evil from
befalling him. The poorer, the weaker, the more
in need of help, the more of a stranger and an alien,
or even of an enemy, that he may happen to be,
the more Christ tells you to regard him as your
neighbour, if only you have the power of helping him.
If ye salute your brethren only, what do ye more
than others? That is, If you help a man because he
is of your own country, or of your own kindred, or
because he is of your side in politics, whether politics
of the Church, or politics of the State, or politics of
the burgh, that is only what it is natural to expect.
But if you help him just because he is a human
being, and in need of some help which you are able
to give, then Christ will say to you, 'Inasmuch as
ye did it unto one of the least of these, ye did it
unto me.'

3. The third precept is, 'Forbid not those that
follow not with you.' If you have strong feelings
or convictions about a matter of Church government,
or the form of a service, or about Church music or
some other detail of arrangement that happens to
be the question of the hour—you do right of course
in following your convictions. But these are not

the greater matters of the Gospel any more than
the tithes of mint and anise and cummin were the
greater matters of the Law. The great matter is
the becoming like to Christ; and whoever in any
body of Christians, or belonging to no body of
Christians at all, is most like to Christ in living
according to justice, mercy, and truth, in loving and
obeying God and doing good to men, that man is
most of a Christian. The true worshippers are those
that worship the Father, not in Jerusalem or Mount
Gerizim, not in a kirk or a school-house, or on a
hill-side, in the old Kirk or the new, with an altar or
without, with printed prayers or prayers made out of
the minister's head, through old traditions or in the
light of new ideas, but—in spirit and in truth.

4. Lastly, 'Have faith in God.' Be thankful to
Him for the past, accept what He is giving in the
present, and trust Him for the time to come. Do
not think that He has been deceiving you, or deceiving the world, because you have to unlearn some
things which you once received as true. All learning must be step by step, and all new truth requires
some veil of ignorance or of imperfect knowledge
to be taken away. The word Revelation means
the removal of the veil. And if some knowledge
which God has vouchsafed of His own ways, or
some higher and purer view of His nature than

those of old time had conceived, compels us to relinquish some cherished doctrine or tradition, we
may find that this is only another illustration of the
words, When the heart shall turn to the Lord, the
veil shall be taken away. We may find that in accept-
ing God's own teachings we have been drawing nearer
to Himself, and when that which once seemed substance, but is now a lifeless husk, is fallen away, we
may become aware for the first time of the power
and glory of the spiritual life within. And the
righteousness and goodness of Almighty God, which
we at one time received as an unintelligible mystery,
may to our newly awakened faith have all the certainty and clearness of intuitive knowledge.

But still the unveiling of Divine truth to human
apprehensions must be a gradual process, and is not
to be completed in this life, and the same St. Paul who
says ' That we all, beholding with open face the glory
of the Lord, are transformed into the same image,
from glory to glory,' had already said to this same
Corinthian Church, ' Now we see through a glass
darkly, but then face to face ; now I know in part,
but then shall I know even as I also am known.' We
must be contented with that measure of knowledge
and certainty which God has really given us. And
if the light which He has vouchsafed to us in the
life and teaching of Christ, and in the lives and
thoughts of righteous and godly men, is not enough

to lead us into the ways of holiness and peace, then neither should we be persuaded to lead better lives and to love truth and goodness, even if the heavens were opened, and we saw the Son of Man sitting on the right hand of God.

SERMON II.

' And he said, Go forth, and stand upon the mount before the
Lord. And, behold, the Lord passed by, and a great and strong
wind rent the mountains, and brake in pieces the rocks before
the Lord; but the Lord was not in the wind: and after the wind
an earthquake; but the Lord was not in the earthquake: and
after the earthquake a fire; but the Lord was not in the fire:
and after the fire a still small voice. And it was so, when Elijah
heard it, that he wrapped his face in his mantle, and went out,
and stood in the entering in of the cave. And, behold, there
came a voice unto him, and said, What doest thou here, Elijah?'
—1 KINGS xix. 11, 12, 13.

IN listening once to the Pentecostal sermon of an
eloquent preacher, I was surprised to find him bent
on identifying spiritual life with the vividness of
religious impressions. Multitudes flocking together
and moved by the voice of one, as the trees of the
wood are moved by the wind: excitement, such as
that which drew men to the Crusades, or to the foundation of religious orders in a former age: feelings
at once intense and widely spread, making crowds

magnetic, and galvanising nations into sudden enthusiasm—such appeared to be the goal of his desire.

The passage which I have read to you from the
story of Elijah came then into my mind, and there
also rose before me the image of One, who in this
was most unlike Elijah, that He did not strive nor
cry, nor cause His voice to be heard in the streets,
not breaking the bruised reed, not quenching the
smoking flax :—of One whose voice never heretofore
prevailed so widely, even over those who still despise
and reject Him, as it prevails to-day.

It seemed to me that in such an ideal as that
which I then heard propounded, the most important
element of the Divine working, if one may say it
reverently, is left out of view. For to measure the
action of the Spirit of God by the intensity of impressions, is to disregard what is of far higher value,
the unaltering power of goodness, the indefeasible
strength of justice, the resistlessness of wisdom, the
might of truth.

In judging of the things of the Spirit, no less
than in other matters, the common mind is prone
to be swayed by signs and marvels that immediately
strike the senses or the imagination, but have little
or no significance for the reason.

And there is one inconvenience attending this habit
of gauging spiritual forces by excitement, that is
especially worth thinking of; I mean its extreme

uncertainty. If that which moves mankind must necessarily be important in the same degree in which it moves them, then (if we look beyond the narrow circle of Christian conventionality) how strange and various are the influences in which we must acknowledge phases of the eternal truth! I do not speak of such far-sweeping movements as Mohammedanism, but in the compass of the literature of the Anglo-Saxon tongue in our own time, how many proofs there are of the wisdom of the command to prove all things, and hold fast the good! Are there not those who through their spoken or written words have an eager following on both sides of the Atlantic, and that amongst ingenuous and untainted minds—who, when their utterances are closely examined, are found to be the upholders of a thinly-veiled animalism—who, through a reaction from some inconvenience of the immediate present, would lead us to break from our inheritance in the past, to cast overboard the slowly-accumulated work of ages, to unite an unhealthy self-consciousness with the unabated grossness of the imaginary primeval man, and to begin again, if we could, with the state of primitive lawlessness, ' ere human statute purged the gentle weal ; ' who would ' take away degree, untune that string,' that we might see, forsooth, whether ' discord followed ' or no ?

If judged only by the test of sincere enthusiasm,

whether in themselves or their followers, such 'voices of the time' are scarcely less potent than that of the evangelical revivalist. It may therefore be not amiss to dwell for a season upon another side of things, which just because it is less obvious, and perhaps also because it has less in common with the genius of oratory, is apt on certain occasions to be ignored.

Let us be sure to give full value to religious feeling. No principle of action can have any power, unless it has sunk deeply into the heart. However much we may value 'dry light,' we know that its motive force is as nothing until it is plunged in the atmosphere of human experience, of hunger and fulness, of desires and fears, of affection and aversion. But the question before us is not that between head-knowledge and heart-experience; it is rather the contrast which arises, in comparing amongst themselves those influences which affect the whole man, between what is strong and what is lasting, what is vehement and what is deep, what is immediately operative and what is far-reaching in its results. And the resulting lesson is the same that was taught to Elijah, a lesson of faith and patience, of endurance and hope; that what is now spoken to the ear in closets will one day be proclaimed upon the house-tops, and that whatever grains of truth and good have already become the possession of a few, will one day be enjoyed without wonder and without mistrust as a part of the growing inheritance of humanity.

> ' The seed,
> The little seed they laughed at in the dark,
> Has risen and cleft the soil, and grown a bulk
> Of spanless girth, that lays on every side
> A thousand arms and reaches to the sun.
>
> .   .   .   .   .   .
>
> A night of Summer from the heat, a breadth
> Of Autumn, dropping fruits of power, and rolled
> With music in the growing breeze of Time.'

A lesson of faith and patience, but not of indolent ' quietism ;' not of careless ' *laissez-faire*,' not of selfish 'non-intervention.'   Did the still small voice tell Elijah to withhold his message, to refrain from action?   Nay, but to speak although misunderstood, to act for the generation that should come after him—to anoint Hazael king over Syria, to anoint Elisha prophet in his room.   Though he were a voice in the desert, yet should his words not fall to the ground; though he alone remained a prophet of the Lord, yet the word of the Lord which he had spoken should stand firm.

The truth implied in this, like all religious truths, is a comprehensive one, and has many analogies in the narrower spheres of human experience.   In these the universal truth may be seen reflected, as in a mirror.

Who writes the history of a political revolution? Not he who depicts the scenes of agony and carnage accompanying the national convulsion—not he who describes, however vividly, the characters of the chief agents in the days of terror — but rather he who traces the slow-paced movements of the national mind, the rising sentiments of aspiration or of resentment, that, having found utterance through some deep spirit, had sunk into the heart of a whole people; and as the snow is gathered flake by flake, amassed by frosts or driven by the storm, until the avalanche is awakened by some morning sun, so

'Thought by thought was piled, till some great truth
Was loosened, and the nations echoed round.'

Where do we look for the origin of other social changes that are less violent and more obviously beneficial? To the agitation of the years preceding legislation, to the meetings of mobs, the eloquence of local orators, the contention at polling-booths through the length and breadth of the land? Or again, to the panting noise of the first engine on the Liverpool and Manchester line, sending a thrill of wonder through an assembled crowd, and dealing death to some one who in the rashness of inexperience crossed its path? Not so—but in the one case to the quiet study of a plain Scotch Professor, and in the other to the unpretending workshop of a Glasgow mechanician.

What gives their undying value to the best works of poetry and art? Is it the storm of passion which rent the bosoms of their creators asunder, the earthquake of fear and misery which engulfed their lives in ruin, or the fire of remorse which scathed while it purified them? Not any or all of these, but a 'still small voice' of intuitive sympathy which speaks to all men in that solitude where they are least alone—

> 'They haunt the stillness of the breast,
> Imaginations calm and fair,
> The memory, like a cloudless air,
> The conscience, as a sea, at rest.'

Even so it is with those deeper voices which speak to us as religious beings, dependent on Him who is all-wise, all-just, all-kind.

They were first uttered it may be amidst the echoes of some great catastrophe, or the premonitory mutterings of some upheaval still to come : they may have vainly chidden the tempest and rebuked the violence of fire; or they may have been spoken in weakness and fear and in much trembling, with stammering lips and an uncertain tongue; but their whispered sound still reaches all who have an ear to hear, when the noise that heralded their advent is no more, and the elemental strife that drowned them for a while is still.

The true word once spoken never dies: the

righteous life once lived cannot lose its power. Or
if through human frailty some seeds of truth and
goodness sown in former time have been irrecover-
ably lost, yet we trust that the same will come forth
again from the infinite store.   Could we but apprehend fully what is already set within our ken, we
should have light enough to guide us to the compre-
hension of more and more.

Let us take one or two examples from the New
Testament.   There were two of our Lord's Apostles,
amongst those admitted to the closest intimacy with
Himself, whom, because of their vehemence, not
without a touch of gentle irony, He named the Sons
of Thunder; who, if He had permitted them, would
have called down fire from heaven to consume some
churlish villagers, even as Elias did.   What remains
to us of their reputed writings?   The Apocalypse,
in which the promises speak far more clearly to our
hearts than the woes; the Gospel and Epistles of
St. John, of which the substance is that God is Love;
whose deep spiritual import is far more felt in the
story of the woman of Samaria, or in the promise of
the Comforter, than in the denunciations of a world
that lieth in wickedness, to which it is hard for us to
give an intelligible or practical meaning.   And the
Epistle of St. James, where once more the denunciations have become strange and inapplicable, while
the exhortations to impartial kindness and to a

faith that worketh by love, the praises of the wisdom that cometh from above and of that true religion which is undefiled before our Heavenly Father, can never lose their force.

Or look for a moment at St. Paul. Many questions that were of burning significance to him have little meaning for us; the oppositions of our age are not the same with which he so heroically strove. But the noble spirit which guided him in the strife, the divine ideas of a redeemed humanity, of a union of all mankind in Christ, of an inward and spiritual law under which order and freedom should be inseparable — these are only now beginning to be apprehended even by theologians; the empire of their influence is still to be. Many winds of doctrine have blown around them—many clouds and storms of controversy have wrapt them from the sight of men : but only when these have passed will they themselves be seen in their simple majesty, and recognised as an eternal possession, not by the Churches only, but by mankind.

And if we think of the life and teaching of Christ Himself, may we not reverently say, that as the highest summits are most conspicuous from afar off, so after we have traversed almost nineteen centuries, the supreme loftiness of His life and teaching is becoming apparent as it was never before? Not in the wars and persecutions that men have waged for His name's sake, not in the grandeur of ceremonial ; not in eloquence, nor in learning, nor in splendour of intellectual power, do we behold the image of Him whose yoke we desire to bear ; but in a spirit that searches all things, yea, the deep things of God, and yet is meek and lowly in heart ; in the simple love of truth wherever it is found, in faithful disinterested effort for the good of men, in moral fearlessness, in unquenchable patience and hope. Seeing as we do that the Gospel which He taught has been so widely acknowledged amongst men—seeing its fruits everywhere around us — we may have confidence that it will prevail more and more, and also that much of what men now disbelieve and esteem lightly will sink into their hearts hereafter.

If we acknowledge and act up to all which we see clearly to be right and true, we may be sure that even through our imperfect means, the word of God shall have course and be glorified : the imperfection, the untruth, will pass ; the truth, whatever it be, will remain.

Thoughts like these are not a ground for sloth, but for activity, whether we are preparing for the work of life or are in the midst of it, at whatever stage we find ourselves in our life-pilgrimage.

To be borne on the deeper tide that flows through the ages, and not on surface currents that shift

as the wind veers—to have a root in the past, to
reach an arm into the future, as becomes a creature
who has a better market for his time than amongst
the excitements of the passing hour—to have a hold
of the great wheel that is going up the hill, and
not of some careering whirligig which will turn
aside no man knows whither—that aim is worth all
prayer and aspiration until we have found it; and if
we are confident that, through God's goodness to us,
we have found it in part, this faith may well inspire
us to unremitting endeavour, to a work of righteousness having the assurance of peace, a work not less
strenuously wrought, because accompanied with the
quietness which is the best sign of strength, and with
the cheerfulness of those whose reward is with them,
though their work is evermore before them.

SERMON III.

'And herein do I exercise myself, to have always a conscience void of offence toward God, and toward men.'—ACTS xxiv. 16.

THESE words were wrung from the Apostle in the supreme crisis of his life. By the men of his own nation, to whom he was ardently devoted, he had been accused to the Gentiles, whom he sought to win to Christ and God, of having been unfaithful to Jehovah, and of profaning the worship of His people. Then he made this avowal of his central belief and hope. 'I confess unto thee, that after the way which they call heresy, so worship I the God of my fathers, believing all things which are written in the law and the prophets: and have hope toward God, which they themselves also allow, that there shall be a resurrection of the dead, both of the just and unjust.' And the same emotional impulse, revealing as it were the inmost core of his individual life, bore him onward to this further utterance, which came if possible from a still more hidden depth,— 'Herein do I exercise myself, to have always a conscience void of offence toward God, and toward men.' Observe how close and natural is the sequence here. First, the frank admission of difference—'after the way which they call heresy.' He will have no false lights, no softening of the truth, no dissembling of discrepancies, no shrinking from the coldness of negation. But then how quickly follows the positive and warm assertion of his faith, which is all the stronger because shaken free from conventional supports, and which, however little they may acknowledge it, he knows to be at one with the deeper mind of his countrymen—'so worship I the God of my fathers.' Further, how inseparable from this faith in God, is that hope toward God, which he also shares with the higher spirits amongst his people, the hope of a future life, of a resurrection and judgment. And then, once more, how closely interwoven with this belief in a God of righteousness, with this looking for a final judgment, with this hope of a world beyond the grave, is the deep consistent purpose which he here acknowledges, this inmost effort of his nature, this permanent motive, this conscious training of the spirit for an eternal prize, for endless participation in the lasting triumph of good !

Of those who have begun life with high aims

and aspirations, there must be many who in the
course of years have at some time or other been
driven to such a vindication of themselves as that
in which St. Paul takes refuge, and they are happy
if they have found the stronghold unimpaired. One,
it may be, is accused of blasphemy or atheism, when
in himself he knows that he is seeking after a purer
and more living communion with the God of righteousness and truth. Another has to bear the suspicion of being unfaithful to his people and country,
or to the Church of his fathers, when he knows that
he is honestly striving for their highest good. Or
he has fallen under some imputation which is heavier
still. In some complication of circumstances he may
have acted from pure motives, but without regard to
personal consequences. Appearances may be against
him. He may lose valued confidence. He may fall
under the frown of good men. But his heart rises
still more boldly in his self-defence, with the '*de-
mand*' of a good conscience, that in spite of errors
of heart and head, of even culpable blindness, of
that most tragic of all misfortunes, that well-meant
efforts should seem to be the occasion of harm,
there shall still be awarded to him the recognition
that he did not willingly offend; that under all
surface weakness and infirmity there has been ever
present the main intention of his life, the irrepressible effort of the unquenchable though ever-

struggling will, to make the most of opportunity, feeling, power, of the life itself, in seeking to do the will of God and to promote the blessedness of his fellow-men.

And even when the accusing voice is from within, when the sins of a man's youth are lying heavy on him, when he is reaping the harsh fruit of heedless errors, when some mistake of judgment or the swaying of some passionate mood has plunged him overhead in bitterness and self-reproach; if he is to escape despair, if he is still to find in some part of his soul a drop of patience, must not this be the last anchorage of the vexed heart, that in the midst of his very penitence and self-abasement he finds that within him which has throughout been pleading for the higher law, which, though temporarily overborne, has still the promise of more life, and, with God's help, shall yet prevail?

It has been said that good resolutions are apt to have a bad name, that they are thought to imply the absence of good actions. Similarly it may be said that a good intention is apt to be undervalued, because it is so often made the excuse of weakness and error. But there is a true sense in which a pure intention is the very salt of life, being in fact that groundwork of an honest and good heart which our Saviour postulates in the Parable of the Sower, the higher purpose without which there could be no growth at all. Because in youth performance is so disproportioned to aspiration, because we have never fully acted up to our ideal, because we have again and again been lapsed in time and passion, and fallen grievously below our highest aim ; is it therefore nothing that in reviewing a course of ten, of twenty, of thirty years, we should be able to feel that we have on the whole been true to ourselves, to our neighbours, and to our divine and eternal calling, and that we are nearer than when we began to that condition in which

> 'The full-grown will,
> Circled through all experiences, pure law,
> Commeasures perfect freedom'?

I propose then to consider the value of a pure intention in relation (1) to the individual life, (2) to human brotherhood, (3) to faith in God, and (4) in immortality.

1. It is something more than a prudential maxim :

> 'To thine own self be true,
> And it must follow, as the night the day,
> Thou canst not then be false to any man.'

He who in early youth has striven to think of life as a whole — who, amidst superficial distractions and waverings, has never wholly lost the deeper longing after true strength and manhood— who, when overwhelmed with temptations, has still

clung with the tenacity of one drowning to an upward clue—whose inmost thought has been, How
shall I make the most of life? How shall I myself
become a fitting temple for the spirit of holiness
and truth? How shall I earn my own respect in
the long run? He who so questions with himself
has a principle of life and growth in him that must
come to good. He may be long maturing. It sometimes happens that the richest natures are the latest
ripe. Living in a distracted age, some strain of
nobleness may often lead him to follow wandering
fires. When after a long period he looks back, he
may have to regret much waste, he may look wist-
fully at the blank places, where some impracticable
dream had vanished, where some blindness suffered
him to swerve into a hopeless quest: but if this central
purpose has increased, if he sees the same end more
clearly, if his will has gained in firmness and control,
if he finds himself more than ever determined to hold
fast by right, and more than ever driven to press onwards in the path of good; then many errors that
at the time seemed irremediable, many starts and
blenches that once brought him nigh despair, will
appear in the retrospect like the dark rings in the
heart of oak, which preserve, indeed, the trace of
wintry seasons, but take but little from the soundness
of the tree.

And from that point onward—the firm and

temperate will once gained, once proved to be the stronger in some conflict with the lower self—then all that happens from without will only enrich the life. Affections old and new, disappointments, trials, uncertainties, losses, triumphs, all will be woven into the strong and various web, without injuring the harmony of the work.

2. But no life can be completed in isolation. The heightening of self-consciousness is not always an increase of strength, and is too apt to become morbid, if not effeminate. We cannot step off our own shadow, but there is a form of reflection in which this obvious truth, viewed in a kind of second intention, becomes a source of limitation and weakness. From being too passive, men become the victims of a spurious necessity. They dwell upon the truism that action is conditioned by nature and circumstance, until all action is felt to be impossible.

It is true that man cannot alienate his nature; but are volition and reason to be omitted in the estimate of natural capabilities? It is true that choice is limited by circumstances, but it remains choice still.—Now there is a remedy for this weak tendency in the thought of our relation to others, in the sense of brotherhood. We are not honest, if we are not honest to our neighbour. We are not sincere, if we harbour any insincerity in our dealings with him. We cannot be true to ourselves and false to any man. We can form no purpose, we can make no plan of life, which will not affect the happiness and the lives of many others. There are those even in these late days, who, after long brooding over their own weakness and misery, have been suddenly roused to a sense of emancipation and freedom by some strong voice that has told them that they are not alone—that they are partakers in the dignity of a nature that can be only perfected in communion—members of a world-wide fraternity, who, through common impulses, common experiences, common sorrows, are growing up into some higher law. If this be a 'new gospel,' it has some striking affinities to the old one. Only it may not be superfluous to remark, that if these wider aspirations are to be realized, if the high places in this great brotherhood are to be won, it is not merely by some magnetic sympathy or the influence of some personal gift, but by the persistent following of some high purpose clearly seen, and by the purification of inclination and impulse through the deeper sense of right and truth. Much indeed may be accomplished by the very intensity of pure Christian love. And the very strength of human feeling may sometimes contain an enlightening and controlling power. But in almost all feeling there is something that requires correction and moderation, if it is not to perish idly or to have a tragic end. For the moment

of feeling is seldom the moment of action, and how
sad is often the disproportion between the feeling
and the act! But for him who has the firm intent
to live nobly and well, to be strong and faithful
and true, it may indeed have an inspiriting effect,
making life to be more than trebly worth living, when
the clouds are lifted from what seemed the narrow
horizon of his individual being, and he finds himself
marching on as one of 'an exceeding great army,'
who have one cause, one heart, one hope.

3. This fixity of purpose may not in every case
have been consciously grounded on belief in God.
But to have realized it in some measure may
be a great help to us in confirming that belief.
There are two moments in which the belief in
a Supreme Being is most felt by ordinary men : the
moment of extreme peril or temptation, and the
moment of moral triumph. When at some great
cost we have acted firmly according to our sense of
right, when at some critical point the accumulated
thought and will of years has been just strong enough
to bear some exceptional strain, and after months
of darkness and uncertainty the happy issue has at
length justified what seemed a doubtful act; then
the cry of the soul to God, 'I thank Thee, O Father,
Lord of heaven and earth,' is no less unbidden and
no less real than that other cry, 'O wretched man
that I am, who shall deliver me from the body of

this death?' At such times the consciousness of the victory of the higher principle in ourselves passes readily into the consciousness of union with the Divine Will. And as these moments leave their impress, the sense of the growth of a purer life within may become inseparable from the still higher sense that we are living continually in the presence of the Infinite and Eternal Good.

4. For, lastly, this deep consciousness of a true purpose in fulfilling our course, may pass into the felt assurance of participation in the life that cannot die. It is not that we have been working for a reward ; but the work that is its own reward is found to blossom with the hope of immortality. The spirit that has realized itself, that has lived in and for others, that has found rest in God, begins to find it impossible to think itself away. It is not necessary that we should dwell much on this. The thought of duty, and of the claims of other men, the various interests of life, the noble efforts of an honourable career in working for ourselves and all for whom we care, these may fill the heart in ordinary moods ; but there are times when all this would seem an unreal and cruel mockery if it were crossed with the suspicion of death, and there are also times when he who has striven consistently for the right and true finds the sense of an immortal destiny borne in upon him to his unspeakable comfort, 'without the will.'

'Herein,' then, 'let us exercise ourselves,' while we have time. The prize is worth the training, and all who train for it may win. We may be conscious of many failures, of much dangerous weakness; we may be burdened with the consequences of past mistakes, of past sins. Let us not deceive ourselves, but frankly acknowledge the point at which we stand. Only let us be sure of this, that in so far as we have striven heretofore to have a conscience void of offence, in so far as we determine henceforth at any cost to keep the higher way, we have in us an earnest of the blessed life.

. . . . Words are indeed 'weak masters' to affect the springs of action. But by whatever means the lesson of experience is applied, reflection awakened, true purposes confirmed, it may be that something is saved from the sad waste of human powers, something gained from the higher objects of endeavour, some few grains added to the scale of good.

SERMON IV.

FEELING AND ACTION.

'I have shewed you all things, how that so labouring ye ought to strengthen the weak, and to remember the words of the Lord Jesus, How he said, It is more blessed to give than to receive.'— ACTS xx. 35.

CHRISTIANITY is the religion of action, and not of mere feeling. If there be any Christians who would rest their hopes on emotional experience, or who make it their chief aim to cultivate a certain frame of mind, they are falling far short of the ideal that is set before them in the New Testament. Nor can there be a greater misapprehension than to suppose that the spirit of Christ has given sacredness only to the passive virtues. The passive graces may perhaps have been chiefly exemplified in some of the mediæval saints, though even these men, if we could see them as they really were, would often prove to be different from our traditional notions of them : but it would be an error like those we read of in savage tribes, to imagine that the mild and forgiving aspect of the follower of Christ is inconsistent with the most heroic firmness of resolve.

Still it is no less true that Christian action has a basis of feeling. For Christian energy is the direct outcome of Christian faith and love. It is just because that love is so strong, that it cannot remain in the form of feeling, it cannot rest until it has gone forth in act. And Christian love is so strong because it is so pure, because it has risen out of the lower atmosphere, in which affection is mingled with desire, into that higher region where all desire is stifled except the fervent desire for others' good, and where the one ruling element is a beneficent will.

It would be a conception no less unworthy than the former one, to suppose that the Christian heart is cold, that its pulses are languid and feeble, because forsooth it has dominated over selfish passions, and has subordinated the lower to the higher law.

Nor does feeling cease to be human and personal when it becomes Christian. There is, indeed, a difficulty in touching upon this subject, for fear we should blend earthly shadows with the heavenly realities : and this was probably one reason why the authors of the two last revisions of the English Bible substituted 'charity,' a word taken from the Roman Catholic version, for the simpler 'love,' which had obtained in all the previous versions from Tyndale downwards. But although the love of Christ is

wholly separate from much that men call love, yet in
all human affection that deserves the name there is a
germ or promise of that which, in its ultimate purity,
when breathed on from on high, becomes the Christian
love of the brethren and of mankind. Feeling, at least,
gives the material out of which the Christian life has
to be woven ; and if the work has sometimes to be
done by repression and antagonism, there is still a
sort of kindred between the matter and the form.

The life of Christ is indeed so far removed in universal strength and purity from our ordinary life, that
we find it hard to realize that He who healed the
multitudes and scathed the Pharisees with His
rebuke, is the same who ate and drank with publicans
and sinners, who wept at the grave of Lazarus, who,
having loved 'His own that were in the world, loved
them unto the end.

But the example of St. Paul, if less absolutely
perfect and divine, and in some ways less universally
applicable, is perhaps for that very reason more
readily comprehended by us, when we begin to look
into his Epistles for St. Paul himself, and not merely
for a dogmatic system.

In the passage before us we have a very touching
and clearly authentic link between the actual life of
the Apostle and the teaching of his Lord. And in
this parting speech to the Ephesian elders he has
preserved a saying, which gives the most simple and

unforced expression to one of the deepest principles of the life of Christ ; of which, however, the nearest equivalent in the Gospel records is the direct precept given to the Apostles in their first mission : 'Freely ye have received, freely give :'—a saying which strikes the key-note of all the highest feeling, which rescues feeling from effeminacy by directing it into the channel of active energy—a saying, no less applicable to the parts than to the whole of life : 'It is more blessed to give than to receive.'

It is a significant fact that these words of Christ were recalled by the Apostle in the moment of parting. Let us try to place ourselves in the position of those who heard them. Or rather, let us look steadfastly both at him and them.

Like the Master whom he served, his face is set to go towards Jerusalem, though, unlike his Master, he knoweth not the things that will befall him there. No power can withhold him, as once from going forth into the strange Gentile lands, so now from leaving them when they are filled with his friends, from testifying to the Gospel of Christ at Jerusalem and finally at Rome. No force can hinder him : not hatred menacing in front, nor friendship calling from behind. And yet we know something of the tenderness of that spirit. Witness the letter written long afterwards from his Roman prison to his early converts at Philippi—thanking God for every remem-

brance of them, having them in his heart, rejoicing
in the graces they display, willing even to live on in
pain, if it be more needful for them. If he felt thus
towards the Philippians after so many years, what
must he have felt in telling those amongst whom he
had gone in and out for a much longer time than he
ever spent at Philippi, that they all should see his
face no more? Yet no less eagerly than if he were
regardless of them, he goes burning onward on his
fiery way—not fruitlessly, however, but still shedding
blessings on those whom he leaves. Rare union of
strength and sympathy, of zeal and gentleness—what
may it not accomplish where it is found? Do you
suppose that, if the Apostle had expounded with the
most heavenly clearness, with the most irrefragable
logic, the scheme of salvation, the doctrine of
righteousness by faith, or even the calling of the
Gentiles, but had lacked this gift, he would have
made converts and founded Churches, or have won
souls for Christ? It is instructive to look sometimes
even on the greatest prophets from the human side—
not merely to acknowledge the human element in the
Bible (which does not necessarily mean the element
of imperfection), but to trace the working of those
experiences which seem analogous to our own, and
yet are raised and altered in their nature by their
inseparable union with the divine truths, to which
they helped to give free course in the world.

We read of one, who had visions and revelations of the Lord, who was determined to know nothing but Christ crucified, whose spirit bore witness that he and his brethren were the children of God. And, when we look a little closer, it perhaps surprises us to find such an one using the simple and familiar language of the heart. 'We, brethren, being taken from you for a short time in presence, not in heart, endeavoured the more abundantly to see your face with great desire.' 'We were comforted over you in all our affliction and distress.' 'For now we live, if ye stand fast.' 'We were ready to have given you even our own souls, because ye were dear unto us.' 'If I make you sorry, who then is he that maketh me glad?' 'We seek not yours but you.' He who wrote thus knew something of the joys and griefs, the hopes and disappointments, of personal feeling. But all is sublimated and enlarged by the great central devotion to the Divine Saviour, while towards the brethren his love seems to have no limit, but to be almost equally individual and universal.

And now he gives to those who are hanging on his words for the last time, who are ready to fall about his neck, the secret of his own strong life, which is able also to give strength to theirs. Whilst hearing the gospel from his lips, overshadowed by his influence, drinking in his spirit, it was impossible for them to realize the fulness of this blessing. But now that he is to be withdrawn from them, and they are to see his face no more, it may be like a new beginning to them of the life from heaven, if the current that has been day by day filling their hearts can but overflow in a strong and steady stream on one another, on the Church, and on the world.

And this, brethren, is the type of a process that is ever going on. For all of us there is a time to receive, and a time to give, and we are happy if we do not confound them. It is well for those who have been blessed in receiving, if they recognise in time the call to be blessed in giving, and are able to believe that this is the greater blessing.

For there is a degree of selfishness in our individual gladness and sorrow. It is in the very nature of strong feeling to be exclusive of other interests while it lasts. Who is not aware that there is a tinge of selfishness even in the purest joy? Can the children of the bride-chamber weep with them that weep? Do not the mourners seem to them as dead who are burying their dead? Can they rejoice with others who rejoice, or have they room for any joy but one? Can they acknowledge their equality with other men, or believe that there is any happiness like theirs? Do they think that any others have a right to deck themselves with flowers, or to bask in the light that seems to be shining for them alone?

And is not the mourner, in the hour of his

mourning, still more self-absorbed? What are all the sorrows of the world to his? How shallow and meaningless seem to him all the pursuits and interests of other men!

> 'The tempest in his soul
> Doth from his senses take all feeling else
> Save what beats there.'

But then these joys and sorrows are the very woof and warp of life, and it is out of these that all experience is woven. In the deepest natures they have been the deepest, and those who are most capable of them have in the long run the greatest power of doing good—or harm.

And what a tangled and disordered web it often seems! If individual happiness (in one sense) were the end, how unintelligible would the whole appear!

One man has keen longings, whose very utterance echoes through the ages, and the great world pauses breathlessly to read the 'legend of his heart;' but when the flower is seized its bloom is shed, and he is involved in a maze of error that lays him low and stains his name. Another has stretched out his hands in holiest aspiration for a coming hour, and it comes not; or when it comes, through circumstances, or some mood of nature, or that 'strong daughter of the voice of God,' his arms are pinioned to his side.

What then? Is life to be a desert still? Must human feelings always have this devastating force— the land as the garden of Eden before them, and behind them a desolate wilderness? Must the bitterness of cynicism still be the harsh heir of unreasoning hope?

The most destructive powers of nature have been brought partially under the control of man. The sublime challenge, which once expressed so finely the impotence of the creature before his God, 'Canst thou send lightnings, that they may go, and say unto thee, Here we are?' is no longer unanswerable. Man has unravelled the secret of the dark clouds, and has turned their armoury into an engine of beneficent labour.

But who shall tame the lightnings of the human breast? Who shall turn their hidden fires, from being a treasury of wasteful storms, into what they were surely meant to be, an inexhaustible source of endless blessing?

Some look to philosophy for this, others to art.

Moral philosophy tells us, and we do well to listen to her, of the 'autonomy of the will.' And it is a sad day for any of us when he loses faith in this, when he suffers anything to overcloud and hide from him either the supremacy of the moral law or the reality of human freedom. That is to lose at once the compass and the rudder of his course, and to drift helplessly and hopelessly away. When we suffer ourselves to think that our antecedents, or the nature that is given to us at birth, some slumbering gemmule, some irresistible influence, or some unaccountable fatality of circumstances working together with these, must necessarily rule our spirit's destiny, then our foot is upon the verge of a steep decline. Never be this forgotten : the power of choice is ours, at least as surely as we have each a soul.

But human nature is complex, and human characters are diverse, and the ideas of duty and freedom, while they appeal to the practical reason, have often little immediate power upon the heart. They are too abstract, too remote from outward impressions, to be sufficiently operative by themselves.

Still less can art supply the needful charm. Æsthetic culture speaks to us of harmony and proportion in all things, of good taste, of stillness and repose, of the union of various elements in forms of beauty. And such a voice as this may calm and cheer the spirit for a while,—until passion wakens in her might, and then you will seek in vain to 'fetter strong madness with a silken thread, charm ache with air, and agony with words.' And it may be found that the sweetness previously distilled from imagination and fancy has only heaped up fuel for the consuming fire.

We cannot dispense with any aid by which we may hope to conquer in the battle with self : but I believe that we are neglecting the most powerful of all, when we do not listen to the voices that still reach

us through the New Testament and seek to make
our own in practice the example of Christ and of His
greatest followers. I believe that if any one principle
will give peace and strength to the human heart by
which we live, and turn its powers and instincts from
being self-destructive into a universal blessing, it is
this, when received not as a mere sentiment but as an
abiding motive: 'It is more blessed to give than to
receive.'

It is hardly natural that we should learn this all at
once. For most of us it seems to be necessary that
we should receive—ay, and lose, too—before we can
know the blessedness of giving. And yet there are a
few natures, at once passionless and full of human
kindness, who seem carried by an inherent impulse to
be ever ministering to others, in little things if not in
great, who have been almost free from selfish pre-
occupations even from their youth. They have their
own peculiar blessing. But those who have felt and
suffered greatly are, when once they make the turn,
perhaps capable of a kind of service, which is not
otherwise to be attained. Such have often a strange
'power of ministration in them.' When the intensity
of individual joy and sorrow is in the past, it may
often be that the truest life is only to begin. Experience then supplies a measure of human possibilities,
and gives the power of entering into human delight
and pain. Those who have suffered are able to

succour others. He who has been tempted can strengthen his brethren who are tempted. They whose affections have been the deepest will, when they open their eyes and look around them, be most keenly alive to the various wants and claims of all men. The more intense the background, the stronger will be the lines in the front of the picture.

The most lasting happiness of all intercourse lies in giving more than we receive. Then only can the sympathy for which we crave be a source of strength and not of weakness to us, when it is met on our part with active energy, and when it is associated with vitalizing thought. Observe the effect of this in the Apostle St. Paul. What can be stronger than the affection to which he gives continual expression? How fearlessly it goes forth from him, even passing into fondness sometimes. But then, how beneficently active; how completely dominated and controlled by the determination to bear witness to the truth, and to maintain at any cost the freeness of the Gospel; how ready to relinquish all return, all satisfaction except that of knowing that his converts are growing up to the fulness of the stature of Christ. 'All things are for your sakes.' 'For now we live, if ye stand fast in the Lord.'

Within the range of our experience, the nearest approach to that love of the brethren of which the

Apostle speaks, is in the intercourse of Christian friends. Let them hold fast the image that is set before them. It cannot be realized by any warm effusion of feeling, by any words of kindness, but only by the active interchange of the highest gifts, and by the common participation in efforts for the good of men. For Christian love is in danger either of drooping or of deteriorating, unless it is ever taking a wider range. 'If ye salute your brethren only, what reward have ye?' We shall lose nothing, but only gain, by turning away for a time from those of whom we may hope to receive, and 'letting our light shine' on those who can but feebly reflect it back. Then, however we may be sometimes haunted by 'the grief that saps the mind,' our lives will be enlarged and blessed, because they will become the receptacle and medium of that highest blessing, which is increased the more that it is shared.

The great mediæval poet, in whom we still find the best expression of many religious thoughts—for the consecrated and harmonious utterance of our reformed religion is a thing of the future—has given noble expression to this aspect of the Christian ideal. He supposes himself to be thus addressed by his imaginary guide:

> ' " Because are thither pointed your desires,
>   Where by companionship each share is lessened,
>   Envy doth ply the bellows to your sighs.

But if the love of the supernal sphere
  Should upwardly direct your aspiration,
  There would not be that fear within your breast:
For there, as much the more as one saith *Our*,
  So much the more of good each one possesses,
  And more of charity in that cloister burns."
" I am more hungering to be satisfied,"
  I said, "than if I had before been silent,
  And more of doubt within my mind I gather.
How can it be that boon distributed
  The more possessors can more wealthy make
  Therein, than if by few it were possessed ? "
And he to me: " Because thou fixest still
  Thy mind entirely upon earthly things,
  Thou pluckest darkness from the very light.
The goodness infinite and ineffable
  Which is above there, runneth unto love,
  As to a lucid body comes the sunbeam.
So much it gives itself as it finds ardour:
  So that as far as charity extends,
  O'er it increases the Eternal Valour.
And the more people thitherward aspire
  More are there to love well, and more they love there,
  And, as a mirror, one reflects the other." '
                    Dante (Longfellow's Translation).

In conclusion, let it be observed that the grace of
which we have been speaking can never flourish, if
it be separated from truth and right. Woe is unto
us, if, out of any personal respect, however near to
us, however sacred, we remove by a hair-breadth the
landmarks which are set by Eternal Justice, or dis-
semble our knowledge of any truth. Woe unto us,
if, out of any weakness, we *give*, where to give is to

take away, if we allow any sympathy to cloud from us and others the celestial light that shines within.

But doubly blessed, if, while holding fast by judgment and justice, and daily winning more of truth, we hold and win them not for ourselves alone.

St. Paul has said that of his triad of abiding graces, faith, hope, and love, the greatest is love. There is another triad in which some might venture to sum up the principles of the blessed Life—Love, Right, and Truth. We dare not say that any one of these is greater than the other two; but one thing may be fearlessly affirmed,—that in their perfect realization they are inseparable.

SERMON V.

'That there should be no schism in the body; but that the members should have the same care one for another. And whether one member suffer, all the members suffer with it; or one member be honoured, all the members rejoice with it. Now ye are the body of Christ, and members in particular.'— 1 COR. xii. 25–27.

To have believed in Christ, is to believe in the endless progress of mankind. To have seen Him as He is, is to have seen the universal advent of the kingdom of God.

In the gospel account of the transfiguration there is a striking contrast, which has been rendered visibly in the great masterpiece of Italian art, between the serene mountain height, where the Saviour of mankind in unearthly radiance is holding converse with the law-giver and the prophet, and the widely different scene upon the plain, amongst the perverse multitude. There His disciples, weak in faith, have in vain sought to heal the demoniac, who is seen foaming and struggling in their midst.

And there is a similar contrast, which is ever being renewed, between the ideal image of a redeemed humanity, which from time to time the holiest men have seen—the image of a Church without spot or blemish, of a new Jerusalem, of a city or common-wealth of God—and the actual condition of the world, or of a church, or congregation, or city, or neighbourhood. as this is seen in the common daylight of experience at a particular time.

Men are tempted to think that there is no relation between yonder pattern in the heavens, and this feeble and scattered flock—between that spiritual communion, and this broken and divided intercourse of sin-worn men.

And yet, wide as the gulf appears, there is a way between them, and the form that is seen ascending heavenwards, and descending earthwards, is not that of an angel, nor of any mere idea or imagining, but of the Son of Man.

This contrast between the ideal and actual aspect of the Christian Church appears very strikingly in St. Paul's way of speaking to the congregation of believers at Corinth.

In a city, which in the ancient sense could hardly be called any more a city, where the corporate life of proud free-born citizens had been succeeded by a mixed multitude of natives, foreigners, and freedmen, in the chief market of a conquered people ; a handful of Jews, and a somewhat greater number of so-called Greeks, many of whom either were, or had been, Roman slaves,—a medley of persons insignificant in number and position,—had been drawn together by the teaching of St. Paul, and had formed themselves into a community, which to an outward observer would appear to be half-way between a Jewish synagogue and a philosophical or rhetorical school. This community was no sooner founded than it appeared to split asunder into three or four different sects ; and these, while bitterly contending with each other on points of doctrine, yet for a while seemed to agree in countenancing a moral offence which, in the proverbially licentious city of Corinth, was an unheard-of scandal.

To that little community, so outwardly feeble, so distracted, so clouded with shame, St. Paul writes in language which might seem exaggerated if applied to the most flourishing of religious orders or churches. ' I thank my God for the grace of God which is given you by Jesus Christ : that in every thing ye are enriched by Him, in all utterance and in all knowledge, so that ye come behind in no gift, waiting for the coming of our Lord Jesus Christ, who shall also confirm you to the end, that ye may be blameless in the day of our Lord Jesus Christ.'

Yet these words are far from being unreal. They come straight from the Apostle's inmost heart. They are inspired by the prophetic vision of hope and love.

And of this ideal image which St. Paul sets before his friends, as well to kindle and guide their aspirations as to express his own, one prominent feature, perhaps brought into prominence by the very feeling that it was imperfectly realized, is the idea of corporate unity. That 'as the body is one, and hath many members, and all the members of that one body, being many, are one body : so also is Christ. For by one Spirit are we all baptized into one body, whether we be Jews or Gentiles, whether we be bond or free ; and have all been made to drink into one Spirit.'

This is probably the first complete utterance of this great thought, which the Apostle had already touched upon in writing to the Galatians—'There is neither Jew nor Greek, there is neither bond nor free : for ye are all one in Christ Jesus :' and which he expanded afterwards in counselling the Romans to humility, and the Ephesians to truthfulness. It is in his dealing with the Corinthian Church that the Apostle of freedom becomes the Apostle of order ; and he whose thought is ever most luminous when his whole being is fused in some strong feeling, developed for the first time in full proportions the conception in which the ideas of freedom and order are happily combined : 'that, as we have many members in one body, and all members have not the same office, so we, being many, are one body in Christ, and every one members one of another.'

To this aspect of the Christian life I now proceed to direct your attention.

And first, I will notice two kinds of objection to which every application of this text to modern life is liable. Secondly, I will try to guard against misconceptions and false or spurious applications of the truth which is here expressed. And thirdly, I will endeavour to draw out the meaning in which I believe that St. Paul's words are of lasting and endless value.

I. The two kinds of objection may be thus briefly stated. First, it may be said, the notion of a corporate unity or common life is one which it is impossible ever to realize. And, secondly, it may be urged, even were it possible, it is undesirable in the present stage of progress.

1. Is it not mockery, some one may ask, to speak of harmony and order to a society such as ours, so unequal in conditions, so jarring in interests, so divided between the superficial and the narrow? Do not the coarser natures predominate in any society of men? Are not the refined and thoughtful natures isolated or overborne, if they are not even carried away? Are not class demarcations permanent, while the occasions which draw together those of different classes

are accidental and temporary? What influence can hope to overcome the conventional limitations, so trifling in themselves, but reinforced by the dead weight of long association and habit; these barriers of empty air which tend continually to widen the interval between man and man? What hope is there of bringing all men into one body, when even good men fail to understand each other? Are not personal antipathies mightier to separate, than any moral force we know of is powerful to combine; unless among moral powers be reckoned the power of hatred, which unites men for retaliation and oppression, or the power of a common interest, which draws one class together against another class, and is only a magnified selfishness after all? How can there be communion and fellowship, while men think so much of their rights and so little of their duties? As to taking an interest in our neighbours, as to caring for the things of others, what else are we doing every day? But what a shallow interest! How little enlightened by sympathy! How feebly stimulated by love! How little guided by the sense of truth and good! How much determined by the mere necessity of amusing a vacant mind! And while we lament the prevalence of vices that weaken character and make ingenuous confidence impossible, is not the very strength of individual character in many cases counter-active to harmony?

Might not one, casting his eye over the complex and various but slight and flimsy texture of modern life, be inclined to think that while the bands that once held men together are being loosened, there is no appearance of any more comprehensive bond, which might reunite the scattered elements, and give hope of the ultimate reconstruction of society?

2. And here the second objector will press in, and say that society is very well as it is, and that we mistake our age in seeking for the chimera of spiritual unity. Not unity, he will say, but individuality, is the aim of Protestantism. Individual independence is the ideal of the modern Briton ; you should recognize and accept this tendency. Cease to swim against the tide, and all will go well. The old bonds are falling away, and it is time they should, for the human spirit is outgrowing them, and the strong man, becoming conscious of his strength, is breaking them ' as a thread of tow is broken when it toucheth the fire.' But leave nature to itself, and it will not go so very far wrong. Men, after all, will learn from experience, which is the only sure teacher. A common life is no less a fiction than a corporate conscience. Let each obey his individual reason : or, in other words, Let every man do what is right in his own eyes.

Now both these objections have an element of truth in them, in so far as they are statements of fact.

But the first, in dwelling on the distractions of the present age, ignores the deeper tendencies which are already working below the surface of society; and the second, in pointing to the inefficacy of external organizations, ignores the possibility of a higher than the merely outward unity, an inward harmony in which order is the result of freedom. It does not follow, because men differ endlessly about traditions or about new ideas, that there are no deep principles of truth and life, to which even unconsciously they are yielding allegiance in common: nor because of the increasing claims of individual freedom does it at all follow that the Spirit is to cease to strive with men. If authority and positive rules of life are losing something of their binding power, the voice of reason should be more distinctly heard; and the heart that is emancipated from the control of force is to be drawn by a yet stronger necessity, even by the cords of love.

When human nature is regarded calmly with true sympathy, much appears that was hidden from the cynical or impatient or desponding eye; or rather, the same signs are differently interpreted. For example, class interests are seen to arise in part from the tendency of men to cling to those whom they best know, and amongst whom they have been brought up. Class resentments are observed to flow from the disappointment of possibilities of kindliness between

human beings who are artificially separated. Cen-
soriousness springs from a genuine care for others,
though that care may be unenlightened and mis-
directed. Revenge has been called wild justice, and
the same is true of civic turbulence and rebellion.
Even human hatred, when rightly weighed, is often
found to be but a perverted love; and the idlest
conventionalities of fashion bear continual witness to
the desire of unity.

And as to those sectarian differences in religion
which on many grounds we may justly deplore, what
is the simple fact? Is it not that we have amongst
us so many hearths or homes of spiritual warmth and
light, round each of which the members cling together
with a sort of family affection, and which have extended to most of us, when we most needed it, a
fostering and protecting care? And is there not
amongst them all a growing consciousness of essential
truths held in common, of common aspirations as
well as common difficulties; of a unity underlying
the diversity? When we consider these things, or
when we reflect on some contemporary act of heroism
and self-renunciation, reviving hopes for the future of
our race, and putting our selfish cares and bickerings
to shame, we shall cease to think either that the
belief in universal communion is a mere dream, or
that individualism is the last word of progress. And
at the same time our idea of communion, or of a

corporate life, is already expanded and enlarged, so as to make ample room for individual freedom.

II. This will appear more evidently when we look for a moment at the second part of our subject—the possible misapplications of St. Paul's image of the 'many members in one body.' These arise chiefly from men's attempting to embody directly and immediately their own conception of this ideal communion, an attempt which is sure to issue in the too formal and external apprehension of the ideal itself.

The longing of mankind to realize community of life finds expression in some actual organization which is the symbol to them of that perfection after which they long. The 'State' was such a symbol to the ancient world, as the Catholic Church has been to the modern, and as some dream of socialism is to many in the present time. But after a while it is found that there are elements of growing life which are not taken up into the symbol: the organization becomes a rigid framework, in which vitality and growth are at an end; and those who had once seemed to rest harmoniously in the same sphere together have become two nations struggling for mastery, the one narrowing all thought and action within the limits of the dead or dying form, the other bursting forms asunder with the aimless strivings of young and untried powers. Thus order is divorced from freedom, and freedom from order, and both are crippled or destroyed.

So hard is it in faith and practice to keep fast hold upon the simple truth, that the progress of a race of moral beings is at once infinite in possibilities and actually gradual and slow. The rule is simple, and yet most difficult to carry out in action, to keep the eye steadily fixed on that perfection which is our ultimate aim, and at the same time to mark carefully the point at which we have arrived—forgetting the things which are behind, to press forward to the things before, towards the mark of the prize of our high calling — nevertheless, whereto we have attained, to walk by the same rule, to mind the same thing.

III. Thus by a natural transition we are brought back to our main subject—the hope of the Christian, as centering in the ultimate universality of communion in all things good and true.

We believe that we and all conscious beings are comprehended in one mighty spiritual order, and that God is daily educating us, through joy and sorrow, through blessedness and retribution, to know more and more of our relations to other spirits and to Himself. The more we learn of these in thought and will, the larger becomes the sphere within which we freely act, and the more orderly becomes the complex movement of our lives. The orbit of our free activity

is enlarged, and also wavers less from the plane of
universal good. In that far-off consummation, towards
which all are being drawn, we shall indeed be many
members in one body, each full of life and ministering
to the life of others, not harming or hindering each
other any more, but each, in that true obedience which
is perfect freedom, 'according to the effectual working
in the measure of every part, making increase of the
body unto the edifying of itself in love.'

For without others we cannot be made perfect.
And it is from losing sight of this, that the aspiration
after holiness has often been so ineffectual. To many
who have sought the vision of the blessed life, 'the
chance of noble deeds has come and gone unchal-
lenged, while they followed wandering fires, lost in
the quagmire.' The true scope of Christian aspiration
is not individual salvation, or even individual sanctity,
not that a few may be crowned hereafter in a spiritual
city far away, but that 'all may come in the unity of
the faith and of the knowledge of the Son of God,
unto a perfect man, unto the measure of the stature
of the fulness of Christ.'

This consummation of the divine order is, however,
almost infinitely remote, and can only be grasped
at all by us in moments of exceptional illumination.
There are lesser unities to which we temporarily
belong, and which may be regarded as nurseries and
seed-grounds, in which the soul is being prepared for

the citizenship above. 'We have a place in the eternal order:' that is a hard saying. 'We are members of the great human brotherhood:' the view is too extensive to touch us vividly. But we are members of a nation, of a civic community, of a congregation, of a profession, of a university: these are considerations which come home to us at once, reminding us of familiar duties and relationships, which are quite definite, which lie very near to us, and are exemplifications of the higher truth that all men are members one of another. There is such a thing as Christian public spirit. For it may be said, If you do not give your love and service to that community to which you visibly belong, how can you be a loyal member of the spiritual community? Or how can those divine gifts of faith and hope and love be exercised, or have any working, unless they have their fulfilment in those human relationships and in that daily intercourse in which you engage as the member of a particular community?

Here also there are many members and one body, diversity of characters and gifts, not incapable of together 'striking a harmony;' each having a separate work and calling, yet each having a vital interest in the life and in the work of all.

The mere act of bringing men together in a society may sometimes be conducive to evil as well as to good. But every society that is formed for

a lawful object is most surely a great opportunity
of good, by intensifying the consciousness of human
fellowship and drawing out much natural kindness,
and also by giving a wider range to the practical
working of the great principles of justice, truth,
and love.

He who truly feels his membership in a community
whose objects are not inconsistent with the growth of
the kingdom of God, has his powers and sympathies
greatly quickened and aroused. Nothing that affects
the good of that community as a whole, or any good
of an individual that has any bearing on that final
good, can be a matter of indifference to him. And
by the good of a community I do not mean the
maintenance of traditional privileges, which may
sometimes hinder as well as advance the corporate
life; nor yet the combined action of any separate
part. The good of a community is its most perfect
and uninterrupted energy in the accomplishment of
the end for which it exists. On that chief end every
true member of the community will steadfastly fix
his eye, and in the light of this he will first of all
do faithfully and intently his own proper work. The
efficiency of every part is the first requisite to the
efficiency of the whole. But then he will also regard
with real interest, in a liberal and ungrudging spirit,
the work and the success of others — like charity
rejoicing in the truth. That is a noble saying of

Plato's—'He that striveth to excel, but grudgeth not his neighbour's welfare, increaseth the city—vying with all, but envying none.' Further, he will not rest while there is hope of amending any evil or of advancing any good. Not seeking favour from man, he may often speak unwelcome truth, or disturb a comfortable repose. His aim is not to keep things smooth, or to keep things quiet, but to bring things right.

Lastly, he will honour above all else, even when conflicting with the apparent interest of his society, the great things of the law, righteousness, mercy, and truth. For these are the universal bonds of all society, without which all human association must come to nought. These do not so much bind, as draw mankind together by an irresistible force, that is above all compulsion, in heartfelt unanimity and active harmony.

And if, in the dust and stir of earthly strife, these greater things become obscured, and we are tempted to set a disproportionate value on inferior objects, it is ours to clear our vision and to calm our will by learning ever anew from Christ. We need not, like some of old, to look for a pattern of the true life in some distant heaven. The true life has been lived on earth: and He who so lived has been taken from the earth only that He may draw all men unto Him. While we rest our lives on His, we

feel a confidence not to be disturbed that God
wills the improvement of our race, and that His
thoughts towards all His creatures, notwithstanding
some appearances to the contrary, are thoughts of
peace.

SERMON VI.

' How can ye believe, which receive honour one of another, and seek not the honour which cometh from God only ? '— JOHN v. 44.

THERE are sayings of Christ, which we are all ready enough to receive as we read them in the Bible, but when we begin to think honestly and sincerely of acting on them and framing our lives according to them, the heart is found to murmur, ' These are hard sayings, who can hear them ? ' Nor is it enough to say that times are altered since He thus spoke, for the very force of these sayings lies in the contrast which they present, not to the life of our time only, but to the common life of men in every time. They are certainly not more opposed to the spirit of Christian society than they were to that of the Pharisees, in whose presence many of them were spoken.

Now there are *two* ways of regarding such words of Christian prophecy, which I cannot but think erroneous. The one mode is to explain them away :

to round off the corners, and smooth the characteristic outline, until they fit the habitual mould of our
ordinary thinking. Look, for instance, at the precept, 'Take no thought for the morrow.' It is easy
to show that 'thought' here means carefulness or
anxiety. And so far well. But if we go on to argue
that our Lord only meant to discourage that brooding despondency which is not only destructive to
inward peace but also fatal to success in life, the
counsel of perfection is lowered into a mere prudential maxim, consistent with any amount of world-
liness. Others again will push the same literal
method of interpretation to a different conclusion.
It might be well, say they, to be as the lilies that
neither toil nor spin, amongst a pastoral people and
in the serene Eastern clime: but how glaringly inconsistent with that industrial order which experience
shows to be the will of God concerning us! Thus
single utterances of Christ are misapprehended when
taken apart from the general spirit of His teaching.
But while the human understanding thus wanders
over the surface of the Divine words, simple Christian
hearts are drawing through them from the heart of
Christ the eternal lesson—at once to work and trust,
to cherish a calm, unclouded faith, while doing with
their might the work which is given them to do.

In the number of such hard sayings, at which
some are offended, while others soften them away,

the words of our text are surely to be included. For what, it may be said, can be more innocent than the desire to please? Could it not be shown that this desire has a most necessary use? Why else has it been implanted in the heart? Do not the best men receive genuine stimulus and support from the recognition of their honest efforts, from the sympathy and respect of those amongst whom they live? How much do any of us suppose of gentleness, of courtesy, of self-control, of all that least displeases us in our lives, would have existed in us at all, if we were now, and had always been, absolutely indifferent to what others thought of us? And are there not naturally, in this and every country, certain 'fountains of honour,' which have an undoubted influence, so long as they remain pure, in fostering the seeds of public and private virtue?

Nature and experience alike warn us that these are safeguards not to be despised. Because human nature is frail, the frown of society will often repress evils that would break out regardless of the All-present eye. And because human nature is not wholly bad, but even in the worst state retains much of the capacity of seeing truth and right, human customs, opinions, and traditions, even trivial conventionalities, often come to us with some shadow of a higher than human sanction. And human praise may often partially re-echo a Divine blessing.

But he who would know anything of the freedom, strength, and peace of true religion, must train his ear to listen for a tone beyond these voices; he must fix his gaze upon a higher and less wavering standard. Whilst, consciously or unconsciously, we are endeavouring in all we do merely to gain the approbation or to avoid the censure of other men, and while we base our lives on this foundation, we can have no inward conviction that deserves the name of faith, and Christ would tell us that we cannot enter the kingdom of heaven.

Do not our own hearts, if we consult them at some calm moment, tell us the same thing? Are we never troubled by the need of some higher rule of life than is afforded by the opinions and customs of any society of men? Can the soul be really satisfied with a virtue that seeks reward, or with right action that is not done purely for the sake of right?

And if we look away from ourselves to any of the bright examples that, having shone down envy, are set on high to lighten the path of erring men, what do we find? That every great deed, every act that has conferred on our race a permanent blessing, has been done in contravention of dominant opinions, in the face of dislike more or less continued, of misconception and disapproval, and even of disgrace and scorn. And if any say that this may be true of greater souls, but he has no ambition

to be before his age; he may be answered that
the greatness or narrowness of the sphere of action
makes no difference to the principles of moral
and religious life, and there are occasions of trial
and difficulty in which the humblest Christian may
feel the need of being strengthened from on high.

Let us try to enter into these words of Christ :
first, with reference to the circumstances in which
they were spoken; and secondly, in their more general
meaning. We shall then be better able to make use
of this portion of our Lord's teaching for our guidance
and support in life.

I. The sin of the Pharisees who rejected Christ
was no superhuman or miraculous wickedness. The
gospel history would be less instructive to us than
it is, if it were thus wholly separated from the
rest of human things. With whatever meaning it
is said that it was our sin that crucified the Lord,
it was the sin of human beings like ourselves, a sin
of which our common nature is not incapable. Nor
did it arise from a simultaneous impulse of popular
fury, such as may sometimes rise from the depths,
not unaccompanied with a sort of wild justice, and
overspread a nation. His enemies were careful to
take Him in the absence of the multitude. It was
the mistaken fear of a popular movement that pre-
cipitated their act. They argued, not 'He is the
people's enemy,' but 'Have any of the rulers or of the

Pharisees believed in Him?' Their explanation of the number of His disciples was, 'This people that knoweth not the Law are cursed.'

When we look closely at the narrative we seem to trace three chief motives to account for their perversity. First, zeal for the Law; secondly, policy; thirdly, the fear of one another's opinion.

Fanaticism is perhaps responsible for more innocent blood than any other single feeling. But pure fanaticism, if we can imagine such a thing, i.e. mistaken zeal in a good and honest heart, can hardly close the mind to the direct radiance of Divine truth and love. St. Paul before his conversion was a sincere fanatic, if ever there was one, persecuting that way unto the death, binding and delivering into prison both men and women. His zeal upbore him through much cruelty and blinded him against much light, but not against the vision of Christ Himself. He could look on at the stoning of Stephen; he could not resist the words, 'Saul, Saul, why persecutest thou me?'

There was a second principle at work in the minds of the chief priests and scribes, viz. political craft. Who shall say how much in this was patriotism, and how much the selfish wish to maintain the supremacy of their own order? Class selfishness is only one step removed from personal selfishness; for the individual becomes so identified with his

class, in which he is as it were magnified, that he
is affected by all which seems to be against this
single and narrow interest : and this subtle form of
egotism is even less suspected, and therefore more
powerful for harm. Such mixed associations of
patriotism, class interest, and selfish fear, find expression in the words of Caiaphas : 'If we let Him
thus alone, all men will believe on Him, and the
Romans will come and take away our place and
nation.'

But if we pass from the Jewish Sanhedrim as a
body to the individual members of it, do we not
find a third motive giving additional force to the
other two ? To take one instance for all, what made
Nicodemus come to Jesus by night ? What silenced
him, when he began to raise his voice in the cause
of common fairness and honesty, with the taunting
words 'Art thou also of Galilee ?' What but the
respect of persons, the fear of man, the power of
opinion which has its stronghold in the common
need of sympathy — that bond of customs whether
good or bad, which keeps unswept the mountainous
dust of error, and cherishes the form of goodness
from which life has fled, till it corrupts the world?
It was this last motive which our Lord rebuked in
the words, 'How can ye believe, who receive honour
one of another, but seek not the honour that cometh
from God only,' or, as the words might also be

rendered, 'from the one and only God.' Human wishes and opinions are many, divers, transitory, and full of change. But the mind of God is unchangeable: the will of God is one. Hence the steadfastness of the life that is based on the simple determination to do that will, is contrasted with the weakness and vacillation of the life whose only foundation is on the shifting sands of human opinion.

It is a deep remark of some one's that the belief in many gods made unity of life impossible for the Gentile nations. Something like this is true of the individual who seeks to frame his course by the approbation of other men. He may be compared to one who seeks to gain a footing over the heads of a moving crowd.

II. Having so far considered our Lord's words in connexion with the circumstances of the time, we may now try to think of them in their universal import. Nothing that we believe Him to have uttered can be without significance for us, as we endeavour to build our lives on His, and to breathe the spirit of His teaching.

No one can doubt that the approbation and sympathy of others is a great blessing — at some stages in the growth of character, even indispensable. For want of this many a spirit has pined in feebleness that might have gradually been made strong. Our Lord Himself in youth and early manhood grew

in favour with God and also with man. Until
principles are formed and ripened from within, we
need authority and the opinion of those we reverence,
as a sort of outward conscience to support our weak
strivings after goodness and wisdom. Yet even in
the earliest phase of moral life no human being
is absolutely dependent on external circumstances.
If the vegetable germ has the mysterious power
of receiving some elements of the air and moisture
which are ministered to it, and rejecting others;
if mere animal instinct can for the most part discern
food from poison : shall the power of selecting moral
and mental nutriment be denied to the human spirit?
The child knows that its father is wiser than itself
or its companions. It has a true feeling of the
difference between those voices of God in Eden,
which to obey is life, and those which would lead
it forth into some dark region of disobedience and
folly.

The youth is still largely dependent upon others,
the support on which he leans being, however, no
longer that of authority, but of example. This has
often been represented as if he were powerless in
the hands of his fellows, swayed to and fro by every
breath, taking the mould of vice as readily as wax
under the seal. But who, in youth, would have
accepted this account of his own state? Can we
not partly remember how, while conscious of much

weakness, we had a witness in our breast which testified against the errors to which we yielded? Did we not know full well the difference between those examples of strength and nobleness towards which we were powerfully drawn from afar, and the influence of companionship to which, for the moment, we gave way? And, amongst companions, did we not feel the difference between those qualities which we merely liked, and those deeper excellences which we esteemed and loved?

Even childhood and youth therefore are conscious of a higher and a lower standard; and, in so far as they hold to the one and reject the other, in so far as they do fearlessly, in spite of contrary influences, that which they inwardly feel to be right for them (though this 'right' may be determined by human authority or by an imperfect example); in so far they are living by faith and not by sight, and show that inclination to do their Father's will, in reward for which they shall hereafter know of the doctrine and be enabled to discern the very will of God.

But the man is to put away childish things : and though this life of ours is, as we hope and believe, only a childhood in comparison with the next, yet in Christ we have set before us the measure of perfect manhood. The deep repose of His spirit was not broken when the hosannas were hushed, and the voices of hatred and condemnation had prevailed.

When no tongue dared bless Him, He could calmly say, 'I have overcome the world.' When deserted and betrayed, He was not alone, because God was with Him. And this was no arbitrary gift of supreme grace, but a divine consciousness flowing out of His divine life. 'My judgment is just because I seek not mine own will, but the will of the Father which sent me.' 'He that sent me is with me; the Father hath not left me alone, because I do always those things that please Him.'

In this, as in all else, He is our example, and it is a false humility that bids us be contented with any meaner aim. It is indeed no light thing to incur the coldness and disfavour of our brother men— it is a penalty not to be braved for any lower cause than righteousness and truth, for no temporary or selfish end of caprice or passion, but only for that life which is higher than all earthly good. The approbation and sympathy of the better sort of men has even a moral value. It is the counterpoise of mere self-will, the seasoner of common intercourse, a wholesome check on frailty. Yet the moment it is pursued for its own sake, and admitted to the first place in the heart, this desire of approbation becomes a source of manifest infirmity and weakness. For conceive the state of one whose life is built—not on the love of goodness, the beauty of holiness, the sacredness of truth—but on the fear of opinion, the avoidance of censure, the craving for reputation and distinction. Such an one may be exempt from certain gross and common evils; but can he ever accomplish any great or lasting good? And to the heart itself what satisfaction is there, if with a fair outward seeming there is no inward warmth or light, but a cold grey monotony, in which the only shades are due to contrast, and not to the presence of the sun? Is there not a danger even of calling evil good, and good evil? For can it be thought that all possibilities of goodness are summed up in the social code of a single neighbourhood, or of one class of a community of men: or that all truth can be comprised in the currently received opinions of an age and country, or the traditions of a particular Church? There can be no real strength without the power of saying upon occasion, 'We ought to obey God rather than men,' and of standing for a principle of truth or right against the world. Suppose this power, instead of being a rare gift, were common amongst us (and surely all can, if they will, look up to God), it is hardly too much to say that it would renew the face of the world. What tenfold strength would be added to the social bond, if each individual, while moving cheerfully amongst his fellows, were at the same time leaning on the central stay of righteousness and truth! What a flood of light would be poured upon the path of life, if instead of trusting like the foolish virgins to his neighbour's lamp for oil, each had within himself the single eye which makes the whole body to be full of light.

There is a country, we will say, in some hidden tract of Africa, or in one of the planets, or there was in some pre-historic time, in which the citizens sought not honour one of another, but each sought solely for the honour which cometh from the only God. They looked upwards, but not to the high places of the earth: they considered each his neighbour, not with suspicion, or envy, or with self-interested kindness, but for his good to edification, and to provoke one another to love and to good works. And as their sole pre-occupation was the desire of doing those things which pleased the all-loving Father, the heart had full leisure to expand in sympathy and loving-kindness towards every human need. They were not like a shoal of fish whose instinct or necessity is to keep the head up-stream, but like the birds whose freedom of movement is only equalled by their wide range of vision. The rich men of that country could use hospitality, without fearing lest liberality should be mistaken for display: the less wealthy were not tempted to shorten their means of usefulness by spending for the sake of appearance and position. While fully alive and open to human sympathy, every person there was fully engaged, without the fear or desire of human favour, in the service of God and man.

To take the lowest ground, what a saving was there here of human energy! The time and thought that is spent in other lands in the effort to rise, or to win favour, was free to be given to the task of ministering to the wants of all—kindness to those who have need of kindness, society to the lonely, food to the hungry, encouragement to the desponding, strength to the feeble knees. And then how great must have been the mutual confidence of different ranks and classes, if such there were! When all were thinking how they could best show their good-will to others, whether above them or below, they could not have time to think whether others were showing them enough of honour. They walked by the rule of that to which they had attained: and if on any point their thoughts were jarred by honest differences, they could look patiently for the time when God would reveal even this unto them.

The craving for a life of excitement was unknown, for all found joy and satisfaction enough in the work which they were best able to do for one another.

Detraction and calumny could not exist, where there was no motive for pulling others back that men might themselves seem to be going forward.

Nor was the path of life beset with doubt and

uncertainty, to anything like the same extent that
it is with us. For when the false cross-lights and
colourings which are brought in by the respect of
persons, and the desire for external honours, are
removed, it is wonderful how clear and simple many
practical questions of right and wrong are found to
appear, which now seem beset and clouded with
difficulty.

And those who had no silver or gold had
still much to give, viz. their willingness to labour
honestly for the common good.

Lastly, the temptations to untruthfulness which
infest most communities must have been absent there.
For when all felt that they were members one of
another, what motive could prevent any from speaking
truth with his neighbour?

It may be that there is no such land, and that
the idea of such a city is still for us as for the wise
of old 'a pattern laid up in heaven.'

But there is no reason why that ideal should not
be more and more realized, if individual Christians
would set themselves to follow earnestly in the path
where Christ has led, to take up His yoke and learn
of Him. That path may at first seem lonely, but
the most loving heart shall find in it the pain of
isolation compensated with the richest blessing. He
who walks therein will not respond less to sympathy

because he is independent of human favour. In his
turn he will be enabled to strengthen others, and
to be a giver and not a receiver merely. That is
no mere Stoical self-dependence, although the dignity
of the Stoic life may well put many Christians to
shame. The spirit which is untouched by earthly
glory is the reverse of proud. He whose eye is fixed on
the one divine life, cannot but ever feel that he is an
unprofitable servant. He will be too much humbled
by the contemplation, to draw comparisons between
himself and others. Pride is really a sign of weakness
and dependence, of a spirit that after all receiveth
glory of men.

Nor is the Christian ever truly alone or isolated.
He may be accidentally separated in thought and
feeling from those amongst whom he lives, for whom
he labours, whom in the spirit of Christ he loves; but
every Christian act, every conquest of self, every
sacrifice made in a high and noble cause, renews
and binds more closely the links which unite him to
the communion of the body of Christ. Do we not feel
sometimes, even in a human sense, nearer to those
who are far away than to some who are standing
within a few feet of us, conversing with us, looking
us in the face? Like to such a mingled sense of
isolation and communion is the higher experience of
the Christian, as he turns away from earthly praise
to rest in the love of Christ and God, and to receive

in unsuspected retirement that heavenly food in the strength of which he journeys onwards, over rough and smooth places, through cloud and sunshine, towards his Father's home. All innocent earthly satisfaction he receives with a thankful and glad heart. But alike in prosperity and adversity, the inner fountain of his life overflows in cheerful energy and active love Such at least is one aspect of the ideal of the Christian life, which cannot be described, except in language which sounds exaggerated and mystical. Yet, although the sources of life are from above, it is not, as has been sometimes represented, out of harmony with what is good upon this earth—as if neglecting this world for another. It is the fulfilment, not the opposite, of natural life, rejoicing in the open day, embracing with willingness all lower forms of good, and giving them an additional blessing, but all the while keeping unbroken the communion of the saints, and holding converse in heavenly places with Christ.

SERMON VII.

THE BROKEN LIFE.

'We are troubled on every side, yet not distressed; we are perplexed, but not in despair; persecuted, but not forsaken; *cast down, but not destroyed.*'—2 COR. iv. 8, 9.

THE mystery of evil has many aspects. There is one that is contained in that sad word, Waste. The germs of life that wither before they are sprung up, the lives often so full of power and promise that we see cut off in their prime, the gifted minds that are sunk in unconsciousness or madness, the effect of a single error or bosom sin in blighting souls that seemed full of capability for good—these and other instances of waste over which we have no direct control, deserve our serious thought; not only because they are to some degree preventible by combined and enlightened effort, but because they remind us that the world of our experience is only part of a larger scheme, which is imperfectly comprehended by us, extending as it does to all futurity and to another state of being. But there is another consideration that is still more practical, and that comes home to all men individually. How much that was born with each one of us must pass unused and undeveloped into the grave! Who is there who has begun to think, and has passed the entrance on actual life, what man of thirty, what woman of five and twenty, has not already learned to relinquish much that had once seemed possible?

The vision of life in early youth, for those who think and feel, has a unity and completeness, 'as of the body of heaven in his clearness.' Whether the aim of aspiration be the triumph of a single power, or the varied exercise of many, there is a flawless completeness in it, a rounded perfection, which those who have travelled further cannot but envy, if they retain enough of sympathy to perceive it.

It is not always that such aspirations are intrinsically impossible.

The profession on which a young man has set his heart may be really the one best suited to him, and if he might enter on the preparation for it with all the freshness of his untried energies and all the bloom of his enthusiasm, his success might be morally certain, and the natural growth of character assured. But other wills have to be consulted beside his own; there are money difficulties which are thought to be insurmountable; or there is a fear of some loss of caste, or of some problematical moral conse- quences which are apprehended. And so the first flush of hope and resolution is checked by an untimely frost, and the leading sapling is nipt. Will the tree grow straight afterwards? That is the question.

Or the life of the affections has been in some way warped or stunted. Some early disappointment, the discovery of some unknown defect for which no one living is to blame, some hardly avoidable error, some too late awakening, makes us conscious of failure and limitation here, where the longing for the infinite is most insatiable. From this point onwards what is the life to be? Shall it wither as from the shock of a deadly wound, or suffer partial paralysis, or turn to bitterness and take some crooked form; or shall it recover the power of healthy growth, and though maimed outwardly, acquire an increase of sap and richness at the core? That is again the question. And it may often be a question of the wrecking or saving of a life.

These are marked instances of what we all find out at some point in our course—that feeling and energy have to be adapted to circumstance; that while desires and aims may be boundless, opportunity and time and human power are limited; that after all false starts and mistaken efforts, we have still a work to do, a place to fill, a line of action which experience points to as our duty.

And it is here that the difference becomes apparent

between the true and false resolution and enthusiasm. We have attempted the impossible. The possible remains. But does there remain in us the strength and will to do it? We have spent a part of life in gaining our experience, and learning how to live; but have we also spent our strength for nought? Let us not believe it. While there is life there is the power of will, and that is the power of working, or if need be of suffering. Faith and hope may be shaken for a time, but let them not depart from us altogether. Disappointment will have a weakening effect for a while, but it will only be for a while if we have any strength in us.

The effect is various. The more speculative and dreamy temper discovers that the world is out of joint, and begins spinning theories of a new and regenerate condition of society, in which every nature shall grow without painful effort into the fulness of its ideal form. The more practical lose sight of their ideal altogether, and fall into a narrow dull routine; the cares of this world take the place of young enthusiasm, and choke the rise of wider thoughts and sympathies. The bolder nature becomes cynically embittered, the softer loses heart and subsides in caution and timidity.

These are the subterfuges of weakness, and we must arise and shake ourselves from these if we would be spiritually healthy and strong.

Suppose, then, the discovery to have been made, that of many plans, only the one that seemed the least interesting can be pursued ; that of many powers of which we have been conscious, only some of the more ordinary can find their natural fulfilment; that of all to which our hearts once clung, all but some poor fragment has been taken out of reach. Imagine the great soldier, struck down in middle life, and doomed to drag out the rest of his time in feebleness and inaction : the great statesman, incapacitated by the loss of nervous power: the great artist,

> 'Whose light is spent
> Ere half his days in this dark world and wide,
> And that "one talent," which is death to hide,
> Lodged with him useless.'

These are but types of what all at some time have felt—the fading light, the narrowing pathway, the autumnal chill.

What then remains for us? If we are true to ourselves, perhaps the most fruitful portion of our lives. It is true that the desire granted is a tree of life, that there are some kinds of growth which can only come through the intensity or the continuance of joy. But it is also true that still deeper sources of life and growth are opened in times of sorrow and gloom, for those who have recourse to them aright. Let us return to Him, who by the finger of His Providence has shown us the limits of our appointed way. Let us devote ourselves anew to do and suffer according to His will, and we shall find springing by the strait and narrow road many an unlooked-for blessing. Christ said to His disciples, 'Ye shall have houses and brethren and sisters and lands, with tribulations.' And so it is ever said to those who give up their desires willingly at the call of duty. They shall lose nothing, but gain all. Their life shall have an inward completeness, though outwardly it may be

'Cabined, cribbed, confined, bound in.'

For there is no part of life to which there is not applicable the spirit of the whole.

If love and truth, humility and deep contentment be there, if the finite being is rooted in the infinite, there will be enlargement even in the least hopeful lot. The firmness of will that might have led armies may be seen regulating the affairs of a little household; the wisdom that could have governed a kingdom may be given with life-long diligence to a country school; the tenderness and affection which have missed their chosen object, or have been denied their natural outlet, may be diffused in a sort of universal helpfulness and benignity. The gifts that, with concurrent circumstances, might have adorned the literature of a nation, or made a lasting name in painting, or music, or some other path of art, may be concentrated on the training of one or two children, so laying up a store of usefulness for the coming time.

The same energy which in some lives is seen breaking forth victoriously in all the brilliance of success, has wrought not less heroically in others, *underground* as it were, unsuspected and unseen except by very few, in a struggle with adverse fortune or adverse health. Viewed 'under the form of eternity,' the one life is no less complete and no less successful than the other. Both pass into the hidden world with equal gain. And He who sees not as man seeth, before whom both sought to live, shall clothe both spirits alike with the life which both felt to be so imperfectly realized on earth. This hope may be their encouragement now.

> ' While I do my duty,
>   Struggling through the tide ;
> Whisper Thou of beauty,
>   From the other side.'

If there be the fixed determination to do what the hand findeth to do, even though it may seem poor and mean, to do it trusting in the eternal strength and wisdom of Him who ordereth all things according to the good pleasure of His will, we need not fear that any experience, any aspiration, any love, any effort of our past lives will be utterly lost to us. To act in the present is not necessarily to break with the past. The past was not given us to mourn over,

any more than the future is given us merely to dream
over. That treasure-house of recollections, in which
the troublous has become peaceful, and all excitement
calm, in which sorrow wears a milder aspect, and
earthly joys are purified from the taint of earth, is
is still a part of us, still speaks to us, though not
loudly yet with many voices, for warning and consolation, for instruction and guidance. Experience
cautions us against impossible attempts. The memory
of affection gives a measure of the possibilities of
human kindness, and teaches one out of many ways
of turning

'As the soul knows how
The earthly gift to an end divine.'

We learn to take up mangled matters at the best.
We perhaps find out a way of turning to account
even the accidents of life, and weaving them into the
fabric of our design. And we are happy if, when all
the bright haze has vanished, when all that once held
apart for us the promise of the golden hours has been
taken from our sight, when we have buried many
hopes and bidden farewell to much solid happiness,
we are still as eager to improve the remnant of our
life, to do good to those within our reach, to make
the most of all our powers in doing that which is
given us to do, as when we first took up our pilgrim
staff in all the exhilaration of youthful ardour; as

when we first saw the heavenly city from the delectable mountains, and thought little enough of the dark valley and of the weariness of the way.

Nor is experience, whether of success or failure, ever profitable for ourselves alone. The narrowest and most deserted life need not be lived wholly in isolation. If failure and sorrow have left the heart still fresh and sweet, as it will be if it have clung to a divine support; then, wherever there are human beings, a way will be found of pouring the oil of consolation and the wine of gladness into other lives. The longer we live the more practical becomes our Saviour's answer to the question, 'Who is my neighbour?' If we have ever cared to know it, we need not go far away to find those who may be the better for us. Have we not seen lives fastened to one spot of earth, that have scattered blessings far and wide? It is the Spirit that quickeneth, not opportunity, or wealth, or position, or any outward means.

There is so much that wants doing in the world, so few hitherto who have been roused to do even what they can. It is terrible to think that we may miss doing the little that is laid to our hands. Let us not waste time in vain regrets, or in vague dreams of what experience has clearly shown to be impossible. But let us gather up the fragments that remain. Though sometimes we may be cast down, let us know that we are not destroyed; though we have sometimes fallen, let us trust that we shall not be cast away, for the Lord upholdeth us with His hand.

Let us pray for some of the spirit that was in St. Paul, who, though conscious of being surrounded with infirmities, still pressed onwards towards the prize of his high calling, who—though in bodily presence weak, and in speech contemptible, though foiled and frustrated on every side, though his last years were saddened by the falling away of many on whom he had spent so lavishly of the deep wealth of his affectionate heart—has left an impress on the Church and on the world which in some ways is only now beginning to tell, and who remains to all ages a lasting monument of this truth, that a wandering and broken life may through the overflowings of the Divine Spirit be made a round and perfect whole, and what may seem to many a sadly maimed and shaken existence may be yet in the highest sense worth living.

SERMON VIII.

THINGS GREAT AND SMALL.

1875.

'And his servants came near, and spake unto him, and said, My father, if the prophet had bid thee do some great thing, wouldest thou not have done it? how much rather, when he saith to thee, Wash, and be clean?'—2 KINGS v. 13.

THE history of Naaman, though it only fills one chapter of the Bible, has much that makes it peculiarly attractive. At this distance we may pass lightly over his misfortune and think of his character, which still lives before us in that page, so fiery and generous, so proudly sensitive, and yet so responsive to the voice of reason, till, as we dwell on this, we feel a touching appropriateness in the blessing which he receives, when his flesh comes again like the flesh of a little child. And have we not also felt the impressive contrast of worldly and spiritual grandeur, of that which fills the imagination and that which commands the soul, when the great captain comes with his chariot and his horses and stands before the door of a plain man's dwelling, and the prophet without moving from his seat sends forth his message by another?

It was then that Naaman learnt a lesson which many an ingenuous heart like his has learned through suffering, which some pass through life without learning, that the truest blessings, the truest gifts, are often those which we are tempted to despise as common.

It is a lesson which only experience can teach to those who need it, and yet it is not in vain to repeat it often in a time when it is much forgotten, and when the marvellous, the exciting, the new and striking, are taking the place of the wise and just and true.

We are told that every scribe that is instructed unto the kingdom of heaven is like a man that is an householder, who bringeth out of his treasures things new and old. Yes, but not all new things nor all old things. He must reject and choose, or else why should he have needed instruction? To cling to old things as old things is easy enough for those in whom such is the ruling tendency. To fly forward to embrace novelties, that is easy too, for those who have quick sympathies and a lively imagination. But to prove all things and hold fast the good, to cull the flower of the present without losing the fragrance of the past, to strike root deeply and at the same time to expand into the liberal air, that is not easy, but it is the secret of the higher life.

Amidst the ever-changing forms of human thought and invention, there is something which lasts, something which deceives not, something which palls not on the true appetite, but can comfort men when other joys have left them scorched and sore. How are we to know it? How could we have known it beforehand? That may seem a hard question. But there is a simple, practical answer to it. Look at a little child. Or rather look at one of those who, their lives through, have lived with the simplicity of children. They have been willing to do what their hand found to do, whether it were great or small, they have busied themselves with the duty that was nearest, they have known their calling; and their life has been richer in blessings than that of others, who once seemed to be aiming higher. The honest and good heart, which our Saviour praised, has been wiser than 'the disputer of this world,' and has carried them safely through trials and dangers in which spiritual strength was strained to the uttermost. For true strength is not theirs who are ever striving, but theirs who know the highest when they see it, who have learnt to reject the evil and choose the good, and who in times of darkness can wait patiently, until the day dawn, and the day-star arise upon their path. We cannot all have the searching mind, that sifts the pretences of the age—the imperial reason, in whose presence brilliant folly withers, and every high imagination fades; but we can all seek for that faithful spirit, which is of great price—we can all try to lift our hearts in the pure desire of truth and goodness—we can yield to the promptings of reverence, to the calmness of conviction—we can submit our souls in righteousness to the creating power, which is one with our own higher nature, with all that has ever been of high or holy amongst men, to the serene majesty of truth and right, to the unquenchable glow and radiance of Christian love. These are the great things which outlast the world, this is the well of water that springeth up to everlasting life—but this in our ignorance and blindness, when dazzled by false lights, we are sometimes tempted to despise, and to ask impatiently, whether some thrilling voice of yesterday, or some phantom echo of six hundred years ago (or of two thousand years ago), some headstrong novelty, some monkish or heathenish revival, may not have more regenerating force than those promptings of a pure morality, which have never been quite silent in the heart since man was man. Are not Abana and Pharpar, rivers of Damascus— fountains of the new world or of the old, of America, of France, of Germany, of Papal or of Pagan Rome, of the far East or the far West, of some other planet brought into mysterious converse with our own—are not these better than the waters of Israel? May we not wash in them, and be clean?

This weak tendency has a lowering effect both on faith and practice.

I. Suppose a case in which the decay of some old belief has left a void, at a time perhaps when the heart is otherwise sore. Then are not people apt to yield to that which most excites and moves them, to that which has some peculiar adaptation to their state, to that which by rousing them from torpor seems to give them the assurance of more life? At such times it is hardly possible for some natures to ask for evidence of the new doctrine or the new passion which is creeping into the room left empty by the old. Their old belief was given up as false, and yet the new is accepted by them rather as attractive than as true. But if not true, it will not last or give them peace; and if inconsistent with right, it will lead to suffering. And when the suffering is over, they will be happy, if instead of looking round for some new excitement, or listening what voice is loudest, they can fall back on the few great simple truths which they learned in their childhood and which experience has confirmed—which have a deeper meaning for men when other stays have failed them, and when the things that seemed greater because they were nearer have shrunk to their true measure.

We should be insensible and without the power of growth, if we remained wholly unaffected by the influences which are swaying our generation. Nor can any of these harm us greatly while we keep fast hold of justice, mercy, and truth. Only let us not confuse the aspects of religion with its essence, or mistake a fragment for the whole. Let us not be so absorbed in some passing controversy, as to lose the proportion of our faith, nor let hope fail us because we hear that some things which have been associated with religion, are questioned or denied.

We and all creatures are not the less surrounded and sustained by infinite goodness, wisdom, power, because the manner of our creation and preservation is made the subject of hypothetical inquiry. And if the Christian faith has hitherto been bound up with miracles, and the ancient miracles are now a stumbling-block to the scientific mind, that is no reason why we should cast about for contemporary miracles in evidence of the immortality of the soul. Such evidence is as needless as it is futile. For the being and goodness of God, and the hope of life to come, are not seen by us in the light of sense at all. They are clearest to us, not when our feelings have been excited (for then is there not something which makes us distrust ourselves?) but in moments of calm reason, when we are neither elated nor depressed, but can, dwell with untroubled faith upon the life of Christ

or of those like to Him. Then we ask ourselves, Can
such lives be without a supreme Author? Can they
be mere illusion? Are they like the flower that
blooms and falls? Or are they not like the traveller
of the sky, that is visible to us for some brief period,
but when beyond our ken goes on tracing his vast
orbit through immeasurable time?

Those who need a sensible assurance of their belief
may have recourse to symbolism, if they will. Only
let them not forget how infinitely greater than the
symbol is the thing signified, and let the faith which
leans on symbols still press beyond them to apprehend
the things unseen. Our robust Protestant faith, that
faith which, rather than yield to superstition, allowed
this place to sink to a poor fishing village from a
cathedral city, ought not to require for its support
either the miracle of the mass or the meaner
miracles of so-called spiritualism. If we believe
that God exists, and that He is good, that is a
greater thing than any priesthood, however pure,
than any sacrament, however full of blessing. If
we believe that we are to live on hereafter in the
presence of God, that belief is more powerful than
any sermon—to remind us what manner of persons
we ought to be. And if we are not convinced by the
simple words of Christ himself, when He tells us
that we have a Father in heaven—then neither should
we be persuaded, though one should rise from the

dead, much less by the common wonder-workers either of the Church or of the world. If we cease to rest with simple faith on the invisible God, no visible authority will long give us strength or peace.

II. The Church herself would have more power for good, if she more completely realized those words of her divine Founder, 'Why call ye me Lord, Lord, and do not the things that I say?'—if she taught more boldly that practice rather than worship is the evidence and test of faith.

If the whole power of this vast organization were concentrated on this as the chief end, and not only as one amongst several; if the energies that are now spent on party rivalries and outworn controversies were drawn into one focus with the single aim of lifting the life of man, of continuing the work of Christ in relation to the circumstances of our age, might we not hope for an increase of light and strength such as has been hardly seen?

As things are, the difficulty and the waste of life is rather increased by the irregular, uncertain way in which moral truths, those truths which are the light of all our seeing, are conveyed to men. The good seed is sown accidentally and by the way, together with much that is unessential. Youth listens with a passing awe, but cannot distinguish before experience comes, between the chaff and the grain. Then comes the stranger sowing tares. Some new ideas are in the air, some 'advanced' doctrine of social regeneration, some half-understood conception of individual liberty, or of universal brotherhood, or of human happiness being the test of good. The new half-truth, adorned with all the colours of the time, competes with old impressions, in which great realities are bound up with some things that have become antiquated and others that have been disproved. And if sympathy and personal feeling, the enthusiasm and passion of youth, be on one side, and truth half-stifled on the other side, what is the end to be?

But the moral law is not a word merely, but an eternal power. And if Man fails to teach or learn it rightly, the error is corrected in the providence of God. He imparts the truth to us through suffering. Not that all suffering is directly occasioned by sin— that is a crude doctrine, which the saints of the Old Testament already learnt to renounce. But all transgression of the merciful laws under which we live, whether ignorant or wilful, brings suffering after it: and it may be said that those are happiest to whom the retribution comes most speedily. Thus we learn where our faith has failed, and our hearts are deepened to receive a fuller revelation of God's law. Nor does He teach by suffering alone, but through the peace which comes when we do rightly.

For the best men this is an endless progress, an

education that is never complete. For when the heart is fixed to obey God and to serve man, then those common, familiar lessons which we may have once despised, acquire an infinite meaning. They are the central truths of all, which give harmony and meaning to everything else in life. To have learnt them is to have found rest for the soul: and it is a rest which binds and enables us to labour. For as conscience becomes more enlightened and more wakeful, the word that once seemed cold and poor, that threatened to clip the wings of imagination and to tame enthusiasm—that brief stern name of duty—becomes enlarged so as to be commensurate with perfect freedom.

We may still look up to heights inaccessible to us, on which the great word Sacrifice is written clear. They may at once inspire and humble us. But for ourselves, for most of us, the watchword of life must be the universal, the eternal law of peace, and truth, and charity, the irrevocable, inviolable rule of Christian Duty.

> 'Stern Lawgiver, yet thou dost wear
> The Godhead's most benignant grace,
> Nor know we anything so fair
> As is the smile upon thy face:
> Flowers laugh before thee on their beds,
> And fragrance in thy footing treads;
> Thou dost preserve the stars from wrong:
> And the most ancient heavens, through thee,
>   are fresh and strong.

'To 'humbler functions, awful Power,
  I call thee: I myself commend
Unto thy guidance from this hour;
Oh! let my weakness have an end!
Give unto me, made lowly wise,
  The spirit of self-sacrifice:
The confidence of reason give;
And in the light of truth, thy bondman
          let me live!'

SERMON IX.

HUMAN LIMITATION AND DIVINE BREADTH.

'I have seen an' end of all perfection, but thy commandment is exceeding broad.'—PSALM cxix. 96.

THERE are few words which to the common apprehension are so much alike, and yet convey such different associations, as 'change' and 'progress.' The one so full of sadness, the other of hope. One laden with mourning for the past, the other big with promise for the future : the one all weariness, 'like a spendthrift sigh,' bloodless and pale ; the other instinct with life, and having the earnest of an immortal vigour. 'But oh! the heavy change!' is the plaintive language of regret : 'Eternal process moving on,' is the utterance of joyous aspiration.

And yet there is a close relation between these opposites ; for that is but a shallow progress that is oblivious of the past. Those who are most deeply conscious of the changes in their lives and in the world around them have the greatest share in the promise of the coming time, as land that is ploughed the deepest bears the richest harvest. There is no progress, then, without the consciousness of change. But there is often enough change without progress. Why is this?

Is it not because men fail to apprehend the lesson which the Psalmist learnt from the changefulness of life? 'All things come to an end, but Thy commandment is exceeding broad'—that is, in modern Christian language, 'Amidst all the limitations of nature there is one law which has an infinite working: it is the law of righteousness. And there is one form of life which is exempted from the general condition of decay: it is the life of holiness, truth, and love.' Even the Psalmist's words imply, what Jesus and His Apostles taught with far greater fulness, not only that while man changes, God changes not, but that man may rise out of change in boundless progress, by active obedience to the commandment, that is, by living and practical communion with the divine will.

I purpose briefly to enforce and illustrate this truth: First, with reference to the lives of individuals; Secondly, with reference to the life of communities and Churches.

I. Life may be compared to a various web, in which the bright woof is crossed with many sombre threads; and while the dark warp becomes closer at the further end, the strength of the whole fabric depends in part on the skill and care of the weaver, who is the human soul.

There has been for most of those who hear me, there still is for some, a time of simple, innocent enjoyment, the comparatively unalloyed happiness of early youth, like the mild sunshine of a cloudless morning. There have been, there are, times of a gladness more intense, the consciousness of wakening powers, the joys of friendship or affection, the noon-tide of the heart. Well, we know that this must pass, must become a memory. It is impossible that the young should fully realize this, although the very restlessness of youth has in itself the witness of coming change. But if the voice of experience could reach the yet inexperienced ear, it would plead most earnestly, not with an austere intent to lessen the sum of pleasures, but with the affectionate warning, ' Rejoice, but yet remember the days of darkness, for they shall be many.' In those days it will be of small account whether some particular indulgence was granted or denied; but it will be of the greatest moment that no remorse should mingle with the recollections of earlier days. It will be a mighty source of strength and peace, if, in looking back hereafter on the brightness of these careless hours, you can associate them with acts of truthfulness, generosity, and purity, temptations avoided or over-come, faults deliberately corrected, high resolves for the future and noble impulses overflowing in the intercourse of uncorrupted minds. The hours so spent will be a lasting gain, for though of necessity transient in themselves, they will leave an unfading impress on the heart.

But the days of darkness indeed are many. There is little need to enumerate here the train of human ills. Loss, disappointment, sickness, separation, the death of friends, the infirmity of age, and our own deaths, although there are cases possible in which even nature would not reckon this an evil . . . . .

We need not now dwell on these things, or attempt to play in 'womanish words with that which is so serious.' Each heart knows its own bitterness, with which a stranger dares not meddle, even from afar. Those who would seek relief in the overflow of sympathetic feeling may find in the masterpieces of tragedy and serious fiction the ideal picture of a kindred sorrow. But we are gathered here to help one another, if possible, with Christian counsel; and the question we have to face with regard to the present subject is this: What is the practical religious lesson to be drawn from our experience of the mutability of human things? What is added by Christianity to the impressions of art or the reflections of philosophy on this well-worn theme? Does our religion merely point, like some others, to a compensation in some vague hereafter, or is the heavenly gain which it offers to bring out of earthly loss also immediate and assured? And is the present recompense which it affords a mere soothing anodyne of consolation, or the strength of a new motive, the support of an abiding principle?

Mankind have tried various devices with a view to obviating the great, dark, inevitable fact of human change and loss.

There is the way of forgetfulness, which would hide the darker side of things, as when flowers are planted upon a grave. Time is a great healer; and the rich, they say, have many consolations. As Nature softens the scarped quarry and the broken cliff into likeness with the surrounding world, so Art throws her many-coloured veil over the scars of life. The weary spirit is steeped in visions of beauty. Society, amusement, novelty, wear off the sense of past or coming loss, and so it is imagined the wounded spirit will be restored. Grief has its way, and tears their course, and then the outward influences regain their wonted hold.

Let no one speak lightly of the compensations which God has provided, 'lest the spirit should fail before Him, and the souls which He hath made;' but let it be said at once, this 'flattering unction' has only a temporary power. The soul of man cannot remain in unconsciousness. Life cannot always be passed in mere alternation of transient

I

joys and sorrows, like the ever-recurring cycle of winter and summer, or as light and shadow course each other round the globe. The tree in December may forget the spring, but it cannot be so with man. He looks before and after, and his experience cannot but give birth to reflection. There is that within him which resists all superficial treatment, a questioning spirit that will break forth afresh through the lava-crust of years, asking 'What am I, whence came I, whither must I go?'

Philosophy takes up these questions, to which, however, heathen philosophy failed to give the final answer. She had ample power to prove what experience felt, that 'there is an end of all perfection,' that 'all things come to an end,' but saw not all the breadth of the divine purpose. She was privileged to stand upon the verge, and look forth with hope into the unseen; but, practically, she could but counsel acquiescence in the inevitable. She held up a noble standard of virtue to those who had strength to climb up the steep pathway, but had not faith enough to proclaim the kingdom of heaven to all men.

Christ clearly taught the blessedness of sorrow. 'Blessed are they that mourn.' To endeavour to explain these words will be at the same time to express the Christian view of the transitoriness of all things here.

1. In sorrow we are often best able to realize the love and faithfulness of God. 'In the multitude of the sorrows I had in my heart, Thy comforts have refreshed my soul.' If at other times we have learned to believe in His lovingkindness, the truth then comes home to us most vividly when we are most in need of it, and in the withdrawal of other objects the heart leans unreservedly upon Him. However strange it may appear to mere outward observers, the pious spirit finds cause for the deepest and most unaffected thankfulness in the midst of circumstances which seem full of unmixed bitterness. And the simplest account of this is, that God himself draws near to those who know Him in their time of need. 'When thou goest through the waters, I will be with thee, and through the rivers, they shall not overflow thee.' And thus faith is permanently strengthened. For those who have found God present in the darkness, will know Him in the return of light, and will fear no evil, even when the last shadows fall, for He is with them still.

2. The experience of sorrow gives a deeper and more comprehensive view of the whole meaning and purpose of our existence. The bright veil of daylight is rent and torn away, and we look out on the open heaven. It is as if hitherto we had seen life only from one side, when suddenly the hidden and higher portion is revealed to us. We have a new measure

given us of persons and of actions. The scales have
fallen from our eyes. We learn that we have been
created for nobler ends than mere enjoyment; we
learn the value of a fixed aim in life. Many hollow
places in our past conduct are suddenly made known;
we are humbled into a truer knowledge of ourselves.
There is a dry light in the saddened eye to discern
realities from shadows, the lasting from the transient,
good from evil.

3. The power of sympathy is also increased. The
deeper insight is accompanied by a wider range of
feeling. How much of the active beneficence of the
world, known and unknown, what numberless instances of wise help and counsel, of the rare kindness
that saves and strengthens, have flowed from hidden
springs that have been opened by the mining force
of grief! So St. Paul is heard to say, 'Blessed be
the God and Father of our Lord Jesus Christ, the
Father of mercies and the God of all comfort,
who comforteth us in all our tribulation, that we
may be able to comfort them who are in any
trouble, by the comfort wherewith we ourselves are
comforted of God.'

4. Out of the ashes of sorrow there break forth
new fires of practical devotion. When in the wreck
of earthly hopes we have felt the blessedness of communion with God, the true attitude of a Christian
spirit is expressed in the words, 'Whether we live,

we live unto the Lord, or whether we die, we die
unto the Lord.' If He has still work for us in this
world (and there is no lack of work while there is
strength to do it), we will do it with our might : and
we shall only be spurred to greater effort by our increasing sense of the shortness of our days here. Or
if any feel that their strength is spent, and that
they are no longer to do much in this world ; without yielding morbidly to such a feeling, which is
often illusory, they will be equally resigned to the
divine will.

5. For, lastly, suffering, change, and loss appear
generally to strengthen in reflective minds the hope
of immortality. It is one of the lessons of biography,
that the most thoughtful men of recent times, even
if they had at one time doubted, have cherished this
hope more strongly in their declining years. The
experience of God's unfailing goodness in all the
vicissitudes of this life gives a quiet confidence that
His purpose towards them is not yet all fulfilled,
and that He will still care for them beyond the
grave.

II. The life of a community has often been compared to that of an individual. The resemblance is
necessarily imperfect. No community can have a
unity or continuity of life approaching that of personal consciousness. But the individual and the

community have at least this in common, that they
are alike liable to change. They have a past and
future, and also a present, which is different from
either past or future, while possessing the elements
of both. They have in them the certainty of alteration, the possibilities of progress and decay. They
have also their crises of transition, when old things
are passing,. and the new things are not yet clearly
seen. What is the practical religious lesson for such
a time? How is the reality of progress to be secured? How shall men ensure that change shall
not be decay? It may be answered briefly—By the
candid recognition of facts: by unabated faith in
God and His goodwill to men: and by labouring
honestly, according to the light that is given us, to
promote what seems to us to be the cause of truth
and goodness.

Let us take as an example the changes which are
evidently passing over religious communities in our
own time. How many earnest spirits of our day have
'seen an end of all perfection' in the Churches!
What seemed at one time the embodiment of an
almost inspired wisdom, is now felt to be a burden hard
to bear, unsuited to the age, an artificial hindrance to
growth, and yet well-nigh impossible to modify. The
bonds which unite particular communities become
feebler, as the lines of demarcation between them
are softened away, and begin to have little meaning

except with reference to history. There are some
who simply grieve over these things; others, cling-
ing to the past, and ignoring the deeper tendencies
of the present, seek to re-animate dead or dying
forms; others take refuge in a stoical or epicurean
indifference, refusing to go back or forwards, and
resting in a sort of sceptical conservatism; others
simply congratulate mankind on the spread of tolera-
tion and the decline of superstition.

But if we believe in God's good providence, if we
believe that He is educating us, and ordering all things
towards the promotion of some far-off good, we shall
see in these very changes an opportunity at least of
bringing men nearer to the day when the true worship
of the Father shall be neither in Jerusalem nor in this
mountain, neither in the altar nor in the absence of
an altar, but in spirit and in truth. Is it a hindrance
or a furtherance of Christian communion, when we of
the Episcopalian community in this country are able
to enter into the sorrows and the joys of our Presbyterian fellow-countrymen, to own friendships with
them, or kindred, if so be, without feeling scruples
because they 'follow not with us,' without fearing
for their spiritual welfare on account of some infor-
mality in the administration of a sacrament, or some
flaw in the method of ordination : while both alike are
followers and worshippers of the same Lord, and if
religiously disposed may receive from the same

Scriptures the good news of the abounding grace of God? Is it a hindrance or a help to practical Christianity that the most significant discussions of religious questions in late years have called men's minds away from theological formulas and ecclesiastical traditions, and have fixed them more and more on the person and the words of Christ? And if in all the Churches there are springing up similar difficulties, similar questionings, and even similar novelties of opinion, which begin to absorb attention to the exclusion of the definitions of the sects, is this a cause of despondency for those who believe in a divine providence? Is it not rather cause of hope?

The more we see of the limitation of human things, the breadth and comprehensiveness of the divine purpose becomes more clearly manifest. Human systems come to an end, 'They have their day and cease to be,' but 'Thy commandment is exceeding broad.' All is overborne by the divine obligation of the law of truth and love.

I will venture to say one word in conclusion in application of these remarks to the community to which we belong. The changes of which I have spoken have still left a place for us. There are many persons who from early association or deliberate choice find a comfort in the use of the English liturgy, which they do not find in habitually listening to extempore prayer. There are others who are jealous of what they think harsh doctrines of the divine decrees. There are some also who inherit from the past their attachment to the Scotch Episcopal Church, and who cling to it for its historical antecedents. Our Church will best fulfil her end, if she provides a home in which the religious feelings of these various persons may find healthy nutriment and growth, and if by fostering a genuine and active piety she conciliate the respect and sympathy of the members of other religious communities in this country. The age of proselytism is past: and we may freely set before ourselves at once a less ambitious and a nobler aim. If we are attached to our liturgy, let us prove that ours is a reasonable service, not only by decorum and reverence in the manner of conducting it, but by living in the spirit of our prayers. If we hold ourselves to be free from certain narrownesses or trammels of doctrine, let us show our liberality by living in true Christian fellowship with our neighbours, of whatever sect. If we are each of us seeking earnestly to amend our lives, and to help others as we can, and are looking in every time of need to Him who giveth power to the faint, it is hardly possible that we should meet Sunday after Sunday for the worship of God without some mutual benefit. And this blessing will be more abundant in proportion as we are able to strip off what is unreal and conventional in our religion, all that which cometh to an end, and to base the fabric of our religious life on that simple revelation of God which Christ has given us, and on His new commandment, which is exceeding broad.

SERMON X.

'Endeavouring to keep the unity of the Spirit in the bond of peace.'—EPH. iv. 3.

THE first intention of these words can never lose its value. When they were written, the Christian Church was as much threatened with diverging tendencies as at any later time,—and these were all the more dangerous to peace, because incipient factions were struggling within the still undivided bosom of one community. There were no outward lines of demarcation, but there was the continual tendency for persons to start up and say, 'I am of Paul,' or 'I of Apollos,' to follow some new leader, to be carried away by some new idea, in forgetfulness of the common name by which they were called, and of the one Spirit of which they had drunk at baptism.

Hence the continual exhortations to peace in St. Paul's epistles. And the peace he speaks of is no mere barren conformity, nor the peace of indifference or of compromise, but one which is inseparable from the fulness of the Spirit. The unity of the Spirit is no mere *esprit-de-corps*, or combination of men like-minded for a particular object; but the union of hearts which have been transfigured by the power of love, not to mind their own things, but every man another's wealth, to live for one another and for mankind—as they know the love of Christ which passeth knowledge, so to make all men partakers of that love, which is in its nature expansive, and has power to go forth to all men, because it comes forth immediately from that supreme love, which is one with the highest righteousness and with the highest truth.

In these latter days the living tendencies of former ages have hardened into traditional differences, which though difficult to break through outwardly, are to a great extent felt to be no longer real; while it is hard to trace the tendencies which seem now most living, to any one section of historical Christendom, or even to say that they are distinctively Christian at all. In such an age it is surely well worth while for Christians to endeavour to find in the common and universal elements of Christianity, which are also the deepest elements, a unity of spirit which may hold together men of divers opinions and doctrines in the bond of peace—a spirit which by its very fulness may overflow the barriers of strife and meet in one fruitful vivifying stream.

But there is another application of the words which may naturally occur to us in thinking of our modern

life. Without breaking the analogy of scripture they
may be transferred from the community to the individual. Indeed, we must often take this degree of
liberty, if we are to bring the words of the New
Testament epistles into relation with our own experience at all. For the life of the first believers was
so essentially a corporate life, a life of Churches
rather than of individual men—that precepts given
by the Apostle to them in the aggregate, often need
to be translated into a slightly different language
before they can be appropriated by those who are
living in quite a different condition of society, whose
political and social relations seem to be made for
them, and for whom the great question is the state of
their own hearts and the guidance of their individual
lives. And though such a use of language may be meta-
phorical, yet in the present instance it has a very
real meaning. Is the man at peace with himself; is
he one or many? Are his days linked each to each
in mutual piety? If all is smooth outwardly, is this
the peace of apathy, which is death, or the harmony
of diverse energies in higher life? Questions such
as these may be suggested to each man's conscience
by the words, 'the unity of the Spirit in the bond
of peace,' if they are taken to express the ideal of
an individual life.

I. 'The Spirit bloweth where it listeth.' The

influences, which we recognize as coming to us from above, and which mould our individual being, are often presented to us partially, in fitful succession, and in their first effect seem rather to disturb us than to control. As when the wind strikes upon an Æolian harp, from north, south, east, and west by turns, it seems to be almost matter of accident which chord is made to sound the loudest, and it may well be thought almost impossible that such rude means should ever produce a harmony. Disproportions of all sorts between the inner and the outer life, between aspiration and performance, between inclination and circumstance, between feeling and action, seem continually to break the promise to the hope, and to give assurance of nothing but a jarred and divided being. Perhaps the heart is full of some impossible dream, when through some seeming fatality the man is summoned away by an imperative duty ; perhaps he has endeavoured to act on some generous impulse, and has been foiled and frustrated, through some half-physical weakness, of which he was before-hand profoundly unconscious. The triumph of affection is scared by the spectre of ambition; the path of ambition is crossed by some compelling call on sympathy. There are moments when there is a strain upon us in some one direction, which we are only just able to bear, to be followed perhaps by an equal tension at some opposite point. In the young especially, the co-existence of

diverse movements is often strongly marked, noble
aims and visions from afar off, existing side by side with
weak habits, uncontrolled appetites, and fitful passions.
And yet it is out of such struggling and discordant
elements that the growth towards the ideal life is to be
won. For in all human life and movement that is not
merely a sinking downwards, there is something which
without irreverence may be called a breathing of the
Spirit. And the Spirit must be there, striving with
human infirmity, before the first upward step can be
taken. It is not from the complacent, satisfied, un-
aspiring temper, that the unity of spirit is to be
wrought. There may be unity in such a life, but it is
not the unity of spirit; there may be a sort of peace,
but it is the peace of apathy. That is not the peace
which reflects the image of the early Christian ideal.

II. But when we look back on the struggle after
it is over and the peace is won, we may see the
evidence of the working of something higher still, of
a unifying, harmonizing power, that was less apparent
to us at the time. And we cannot claim that power
to have been our own. 'When I said, My foot hath
slipped, Thy mercy, O Lord, held me up.' There
must ever be much that is mysterious to us in that
which is so much above us. But if we ask ourselves,
for our own future guidance, and that of others, what
consciousness it was that withheld us from this false

step, that impelled us on that mission that has
ended in blessing ; what aim we are to keep before us
if we would preserve that harmony which is true
strength—the answer is after all not very far off,
though it is, and must be, a very general answer :
' Let them not depart from thine eyes, the great
things of the law, justice, mercy, and truth.' Justice :—inclination and opportunity were strong, but
there was the vision of great Justice, dimly seen
weighing in her eternal balance the joy of one or two
against the lasting good of all. Mercy :—the voice of
the world was threatening, the fear of opinion and of
consequences was pressing upon a timid nature ; but
there was a soul to be rescued, a life to be healed,
and the heart could not pause to calculate. Truth :—
there was every motive for dissembling an important
fact, but all personal considerations have been overborne at the strong bidding of the highest reason
and the highest love, and a man has set his face
like a flint, in the simple faith that no real harm
could come to him from the Truth.

And so time after time he may have gradually
attained some measure of the only peace that is worth
having, that peace and inward harmony, which has
been conquered in repeated conflicts with circumstances, and with the illusions of self. Such peace is
synonymous with inward strength, and with true rest;
not the rest of inactivity, but that which springs out

of the consciousness of beneficent power. This is a strength which knows its dependence upon a higher strength, and which rejoices in the belief that it may be privileged to strengthen others with the might wherewith it has itself been strengthened from above.

III. For the 'Divinity that shapes our ends' is no blind destiny descending on us from without, and compelling us we know not whither; nor yet can we admit that 'character is fate,' in the sense that weakness predetermines men to ruin. There is a Spirit witnessing with our spirits that we are the children of God : a Spirit which we may at times identify with our own better nature, but which at other times we feel to be altogether above our individual nature, and in a true sense to have come down on us from on high, not only restraining us from action, but also sometimes impelling us at critical times 'to do things that are rightful, though obscure to judge :' a Spirit of love and truthfulness, which, like a river of the water of life, ministers hope in dark seasons, and suffers not our faith in man to fail : a Spirit in which the love of man has cast out the fear of man, which is far-reaching because it is very strong and pure.

Resolve and analyse this as we may into the countless antecedents of our individual being, we may yet be very sure that in so far as we have realized ourselves in fellowship at all, so far as the chaos of our personal activities has been balanced and controlled for good, so far as we have attained a just command over that in ourselves or our surroundings which was once too strong for us, we have been the recipients of a power which is not our own, which is independent of any earthly origin, above the conditions of time, coming forth from the Eternal.

IV. And in this belief and consciousness the life is at last girded with the bond of peace. It is not that we are less ardent than heretofore, or that we shrink wearily from the war with evil; for we must still be ever pressing on, the more so as our hearts are filled with gratitude to Him who has set our feet upon the rock. That precept is ever ringing in our ears, 'Freely ye have received, freely give.' But a load of oppressive darkness and uncertainty has been removed. We feel as if we need never be greatly troubled about anything, seeing that the experience of the higher life has given us a kind of possession of all things. Doubts that haunted us have been dispelled, contradictions in ourselves and others have been solved, and faith has been enlarged by experience so as to reach into the unseen. Even in this life, with all its bewilderments, distractions,

and sorrows, there are bright intervals in which we
seem to anticipate the time when there shall be

'No fears to beat away, no strife to heal,
  The past unsighed for, and the future sure.'

And though such moments may be few and rare,
and less accessible to some natures than to others,
let the young and aspiring soul be sure of this, that
they do not come by accident or the caprice of fortune. For those who aim at the highest things and
follow them, who are determined to close their minds
to no ray of truth, who mean always to be before all
else single-minded, pure, and upright—though clouds
may overtake them on their way, though a passionate
nature may seize a part of the truth for the whole
and follow diverse objects with alternate warmth,
though the web may seem at some points hopelessly
tangled, yet the end is morally certain. It is certain,
that is to say, for those who live long enough, for
those who have strength enough for the way.

And what of others? Surely the happiest experience is of little use to us if it does not enlarge our
faith. Am I better than my brother man who began
life with higher aims and fewer drawbacks, but was
cut off by some rash accident, or by over-work, or
inevitable sickness, ere he reached his prime ; or than
him whose errors, perhaps not essentially greater
than my own, have 'gone before to judgment,' and

maimed his usefulness; or than him who, foiled by
some constitutional weakness, or some disappointment, or the mistake of another, has never been able
to bring his powers to bear, and has lived a wasted
life? There are brief lives, whose perfect intention
was surely greater than any lower performance;
there are broken lives, which may still be seen, by
those who have an eye for such things, to be climbing
painfully upwards to the light; there are unsuccessful
lives, whose very unworldliness may have made some
who knew them feel that they were too good to be
successful in this world. Much that is dubious and
suspected to us may have a value in the sight of
God; and if His dealings with us have taught us to
believe in His goodness, we shall certainly not believe
in it for ourselves alone, nor shall we find it easy to
believe that all of it that is to be dispensed to
many of our brethren can be seen from this side
of the grave.

Such faith in possibilities is very far from being
a motive for relaxing effort. On the contrary, it is
the strongest motive to be always doing our utmost
on the side of good. No man who has seen the light
will willingly walk on in darkness.

And the vision is twofold. On the one hand, there
is a full and various life, ever welling up in partial
but vivid energies between the darkness and the light,
capable indeed of being turned to evil, but no less

indispensable for the realization of good; and on the other hand, the one divine Spirit of wisdom, justice, and universal love, giving to each of these partial energies its true and lasting value, and drawing all together into beneficent action for the good of all— just as the great sun, from the wild torrent and from the restless deep, from still lake and rolling river, distils the universal blessing of the rain. He who has seen that twofold vision will have the assurance of life and peace.

Life without peace is weakness and chaos; peace without life is nothingness. It is when the two are united, when self-control is not mere self-repression, but the enlightened guidance of an ardent will, that the individual has realized for himself, and will assist his brethren in realizing individually, the ideal which the Apostle set collectively before the early Church— the unity of Spirit in the bond of peace.

SERMON XI.

PLEASURE AND DUTY.

'Rejoice, O young man, in thy youth; and let thy heart cheer thee in the days of thy youth, and walk in the ways of thine heart, and in the sight of thine eyes: but know thou, that for all these things God will bring thee into judgment.'— ECCLES. xi. 9.

IN hearing these words we are apt to ask ourselves, Was the Preacher in earnest, or did he speak ironically? For preaching is commonly regarded as an enemy to joy, and its object is often supposed to be to lay some restraint on natural liberty. And the sad notes of the Hebrew Preacher are so deep in their sadness, that we cannot at once realize the possibility of his entering heartily into simple human pleasures. We confound him with the modern cynic who, in crying 'All is vanity,' professes to have reached the mortal coldness of the heart. We forget that even cynicism may be sometimes the cloak of a tender, shrinking spirit that has been wounded. The proud misanthropist has been known to shed tears over the faithfulness of some humble friend.

In this book of Ecclesiastes it is the sense occasionally manifested of the brightness of human existence which makes the pervading feeling of desolation in it so extremely touching. And generally
it is the wide range of human experience which, with
all its inconsistencies, is fearlessly reflected in the
Bible, that makes this sacred volume so infinitely
more impressive and fruitful in effect than any other
religious writing in the world.

I do not think, therefore, that the Preacher here
means to say, 'However much a young man may
rejoice in youth, yet the days of his sorrow shall
be many; let him walk in the ways of his heart and
in the sight of his eyes, ay, but he shall not escape
judgment.' I believe that it is a truer and more
gentle voice that meets us here. 'Let the young
rejoice in their youth, it is the gift of God; let every
life have its bloom, for God hath made each thing
beautiful in His time; let all make fair and full
use of the degree of liberty and freedom from care
which is given to them, only let young as well as
old have the judgment of God before their eyes.
"Fear God, and keep His commandments," that is
the conclusion of the whole matter. Childhood and
youth are vanity, i. e. they are nothing when they
are over, except in so far as they have been made to
contribute to the store of life something which will
last, some hallowed memory, some pure experience,

some faithful act ; but " the word of the Lord abideth
for ever." Therefore, " Remember now thy Creator in
the days of thy youth," and do not lay up sorrows
for the years to come.'

Whatever may be thought of this interpretation,
the words may be fitly chosen to introduce the consideration of a subject which no Christian teacher can
afford to pass unnoticed in the present day. 'What
does our religion say to us about pleasure?' The
Christianity of Augustine, of St. Francis d'Assisi, of
St. Bernard, when interrogated on this subject, gave
no uncertain sound. Perhaps Luther may have been
said to waver : on this and some other subjects his
heart used to contradict his head ; the voice is that
of freedom, while the hands are still those of ecclesi-
asticism. But if the first reformers relaxed somewhat
of the asceticism of the mediæval Church, the old
hardness and severity were more than restored in
Puritanism, which, like the early monachism, in bearing witness against the corruptions of the world tended
to strain human nature, and to impose a burden
which men could not and would not bear. Every
excess, however well-meant, brings its revenge after
it ; and the Nemesis of all this has long since come ;
although any excess of severity in early Christianity
had been more than justified by the enormities of the
later Roman empire. Traditional Christianity in the
present day hardly touches any problem of casuistry,

hardly professes to be a guide in daily life. Attempts
are made here and there to revive discipline and the
direction of consciences, but the world heeds them
little ; and the sentence in our Prayer-book, in the
service for Ash-Wednesday, that 'the revival of
penance were much to be wished,' has remained a
dead letter, and so is likely to remain. The Church
contents herself for the most part with repeating her
formularies, which the ministers of pleasure are ready
to admit can do no harm, while the great Age goes
on its way.

> 'Yes, we arraign her, but she,
> The weary Titan! with deaf
> Ears, and labour-dimmed eyes,
> Regarding neither to right
> Nor left, goes passively by,
> Staggering on to her goal :
> Bearing on shoulders immense,
> Atlantean, the load,
> Well-nigh not to be borne,
> Of the too vast orb of her fate.'

But an enemy is sowing tares while we sleep. The
effective preachers of asceticism may be easily numbered, and even some of the most effective of them
may be suspected of having a thought behind. There
are some at least who seem to draw vivid pictures of
the dangers of the world, and the evils of sinful pleasures, that by giving men bad consciences they may
drive them to the bosom of the Church. But mean-

while another set of preachers are more effective, for
they evidently mean simply what they say. Time was
when men were content to take their pastime silently,
while the voice of the Church was thundering overhead ; but now the Church is silent, and they take
courage and exhort each other. Human nature, let
loose from the long thraldom, has found a voice, and,
breathing the keen air of freedom, becomes defiant.
In the inebriation of the moment it does not see that
that outward tyrant whom it defies is a spectre of the
past, and that there is another servitude which it
cannot shake off—the inward and unseen fetter of the
eternal law. Were it not for this feature of our time,
the preacher of righteousness would perhaps do better
in leaving this subject alone, for it is in every way
difficult to touch it without doing harm. Spontaneity
is of the very essence of youthful joy, and to introduce self-consciousness either way is like brushing off
the bloom. But when, instead of the beadle gruffly
telling them to leave their play and to move onwards,
the arch-priest of humanity is heard in dulcet tones
inciting his children to their delights—when utilitarian
philosophy has successfully inculcated the maxim
that pleasure is the end of life ; and before the young
man has well asked whether his own pleasure or that
of others is to be his rule, or still less has been able
to forecast the years and balance against the vivid
pleasures of the moment the solid happiness of a life-

time, the sensuous artist, playing on the sensitive organization with a sort of opal spray, has rapt him into Elysium and steeped him in forgetfulness of human care—when this begins to be the prevailing tone, it is time that other voices should be raised. The only cure for the shallow superficial humanism lies in the deeper humanism ; and of the deepest humanity, the chief fountains are ever to be sought for in Christ. In leaving tradition on one side, and going straightway to the New Testament, we have the best hope of finding elements of wisdom which are applicable to our own and every age. Only, the New Testament, like every book, should be read with discrimination. And there is sometimes a fallacy latent under the most sacred names.

Christendom has for eighteen centuries worshipped the cross. It has been to men the symbol of 'the greatest moral act ever done in the world,' and also of the precept of the Redeemer: 'If any man will come after me, let him take up his cross and follow me.' But let us distinguish. Christ would lay no greater burden on us than we can bear, though He would have us remember we have each our burden. He says, 'Take up your cross and follow me,' but He also considers whereof we are made. The leader of an army does not at every moment send every soldier into the hottest of the fight. He knows when his own hour is come, at which he is ready to lay down his life for a sufficient cause; and when his soldiers have been fully trained he will expect a similar devotion from them, to be exhibited according to their circumstances and according to their several powers and aptitudes. The form of the action will differ according to natures and circumstances; the spirit to be displayed ultimately will be the same in all. So the ideal spirit, of which the cross is the symbol, is the same for all Christians; but the forms of action in which it is displayed may be infinitely diverse. Not martyrdom for all—that is quite clear; not utter self-sacrifice for all — certainly not at every moment: but for all, sooner or later, the life for others, the life of giving, the life of self-denying love. We cannot look on Him who is our Leader, and indulge in selfishness or cruelty. But there are simple human pleasures which He does not reprove, though they form no part of the heroic standard.

We can imagine that amongst another people, in a different age, in a different position, the spirit of Christ might have lived longer upon the earth, might have entered into more varied experiences, might have found more of peace and goodwill. But we cannot imagine the spirit of Christ being at any moment disobedient to the voice of God; we cannot imagine Him at any moment withholding any truth, or shrinking from conferring any good on men. The lesson of His life and teaching is perhaps most perfectly expressed

in those few words, 'It is more blessed to give than
to receive.' But even those words imply that, as
Ecclesiastes might have said, there is a time to
receive as well as a time to give ; and in idealizing
the example of Christ we need not lose sight of the
gentleness of His teaching. His hour came because
of the evil, and because His Father called Him to
fight and conquer the evil. But in those eight-and-
twenty years of which we have hardly any record,
in which He grew in favour with God and man, we
have no reason to think that there may not have
been moments in which He seemed at harmony with
the elements surrounding Him. And this is certain,
that He has nowhere condemned what is innocent
in the life of nature. No picture was ever more
untrue than the mediæval image of Christ, the dread-
ful Judge, who needed the intercession of His mother
and the saints to make Him sympathize with human
infirmity. 'Neither do I condemn thee, go and sin
no more.' 'Her sins which are many are forgiven
her, for she loved much.' 'Zacchæus, come down,
for this day I must abide at thine house.' 'I came
not to call the righteous, but sinners to repentance.'
'I will have mercy and not sacrifice.' That is not
the voice of the middle ages.

What then is the Christian application of the words,
'Rejoice, O young man, in thy youth'?

I. They may warn those who have the care of youth not to lay too much upon the young. Sadden not the hearts which God would not make sad. Let there be at least one period of life on which the memory may rest hereafter gladly, a fountain from which the heart may perpetually renew its faith that unalloyed happiness is not unattainable. At the same time let them teach the young to remember judgment, not so much by severe exactions and stern reproofs, though these also may have their place in a wise training, as by making the beauty of righteousness and equity to shine forth in their own conduct, by fairness, by knowledge, by love unfeigned, by pureness, by truth, by heartily encouraging every good disposition, by providing healthy occupations and pursuits, which may lay the foundation of a full life hereafter; and by making it abundantly manifest in their own life and labour, that there are duties which are imperative, and that there is abundance of work in the world which is worth doing.

II. Let the young believe, what all experience shows, that it is possible to rejoice in youth and at the same time to remember judgment. That is an utterly false and sickly teaching which would send young people on a voyage of discovery in search of pleasures, which tells them to live upon excitement. That is the sure road to an age of melancholy and regret, perhaps to an early grave. If he have not the springs of joy within him, he will nowhere find happiness in things without.

'If happiness have not her seat
And centre in the breast,
We may be wise or rich or great,
But never can be blest.
No treasures, no pleasures,
Can make us happy long;
The heart aye's the part aye
That makes us right or wrong.'

It is a more experienced voice which tells those who are restless in the time of youth to seek for work, to labour at some occupation, to find some absorbing interest not of a selfish nature : then when they lift up their eyes from their toil they will find all nature full of brightness. Joy comes unbidden to those who give themselves to duty.

For pleasure is not life, but the reflex and incidental evidence to us of the life that is there. And the fulness of life is not in sensation, but in action. Thought may be prophetic of life, and feeling may be the birth of it; but action is the roof and crown, the realization which brings after it the fulness of joy.

And while there are most certainly springs of gladness, which may prove hereafter to be the means of enriching life, let the heart which thinks it can discern such blessings be very careful in the use of them. How much may depend on the strength or weakness shown in this, the experienced alone can tell.

III. Let the young rejoice in youth; for it is the beginning of all things, it has possibilities which may well seem infinite. 'The time is endless,' said Goethe. And certainly there is infinitely more of time in some lives than in others, if we measure it by the amount that is well employed. But in youth we were learning how to employ it, as we can never learn the same lesson afterwards. We were acquiring a hold over our own powers, which is to stand us in stead during a long lifetime. The strain, the conflict, the dust and strife, the heat and burden of the day, are to come afterwards; meanwhile the young are gathering strength in abundant leisure, that in the evil day they may be able to stand. Let us see that it is strength that they are gathering and not weakness, and then we will not grudge them the brightness of moments which we can never know again. For we cannot say 'The time is endless,' who begin to see the limits of our appointed way. The motto for us is rather 'The time is short,' in which we have to accomplish even the little that is given us to do.

IV. Let not the young be too ready to imagine that they are able to stand alone, and to be a law unto themselves. If the Preacher said (whether seriously or not) 'Walk in the sight of thine eyes,' he was right to add the warning afterwards, 'God will bring thee into judgment.' Youth is always apt

enough to imagine that it has attained to inward
freedom, but never more so than in our day, when
'individualism' has probably reached its furthest point.
Yet even as it is, there is a feeling of modesty and
of frank reliance on others, which is natural to youth,
if not quenched by adverse influences. Do not let
it be so quenched. Liberty is a good thing for all
who have any strength, but arrogance and petulance
are not signs of strength. It is one of the purest
sources of joy in youth that it has the power of leaning
upon an example, of looking up with reverence to
another. It has the belief in human goodness unimpaired. It would be a sad thing if the disintegra-
tion of society were to proceed so far, that even this
feeling lost its freshness. That it may find its true
sphere and object, however, does not depend entirely
upon the young.

But if the young creature is determined to walk,
not by the experience of others, but in the ways of
its heart, and in the sight of its eyes, God will
soon bring it into judgment. Happily for us, we
have not to wait for a future and final day of judgment for the proofs of our own folly. 'Happy are
those to whom Nemesis comes speedily.' Or rather,
happy are those who hear the first hoarse whisper,
and take the warning before the storm is come.
Sooner or later we all find ourselves in the presence
of eternal justice, and the moralizing is done for

us, if we do it not for ourselves. But those are happiest of all in whom the belief has gone before the experience.

V. It would be wrong to forget that there are some to whom youth is not a time of joy: to whom their first severe trials come at a time when they are least able to bear them, a time when to feel sorrow is to think it impossible ever to smile again. It would be mockery to teach them to rejoice, perhaps even to speak to them of joy. But, in fact, life is full of compensations; and though the traces of early sorrow may long remain, yet it may have opened depths within them, which long afterwards may become a source of truest blessing.

Lastly—not to conclude a subject which has been hardly begun, but to end this sermon—let us not think to offer that which is maimed, and call this a reasonable service. Let us all try to make each part of life beautiful in his time, living honestly as in the day, striving after the incorruptible crown, and pressing ever onwards; but not torturing ourselves or others with an ideal of life which has owed its strength to the violence of a twofold reaction, or with an idea of the nature of God which daily experience proves to be untrue, and which, from whencesoever it comes to us, is not the image of the Father of whom Christ told the world, the Father, who clothes the lilies of the field with beauty, who careth for the sparrow, who, not in savage irony but in tender and forbearing mercy, still maketh His sun to rise upon the evil and the good, and sendeth rain upon the just and unjust.

SERMON XII.

TRUE MANLINESS.

'Quit you like men, be strong.'—1 COR. xvi. 13.

SOME of the most striking and memorable words of the Apostle St. Paul are uttered with strange suddenness, amongst the salutations and particular messages, which in his affectionate care he used to pour forth to individuals in the Church to which he had been writing, ere he closed an epistle. Though he was ever present with his absent converts in spirit, it was like a fresh parting from them when, with his heart enlarged towards them after dictating the burning words of his letter, he sat down and added his signature to the scroll or tablet waiting to be dispatched by the hand of some mutual friend, before he returned to his daily task of manual toil, or addressed himself to the spiritual wants of some other community, near or far off, whose burden also lay upon him. And as, in moments of parting, words sometimes fly to the lips unbidden, in which are concentrated the thoughts and feelings of months or years ; so in these closing passages, as the Apostle thinks over one by one the souls who most need his counsel, his deepest aspirations and convictions spring forth anew, and are summed up in a short precept or ejaculation. So in finishing the letter to the Galatians 'with his own hand,' he writes, 'God forbid that I should glory save in the cross of our Lord Jesus Christ. . . . . For in Christ Jesus neither circumcision availeth anything, nor uncircumcision, but a new creature.' And in taking leave of his early converts at Philippi, after special exhortations to Euodias and Syntyche and others, he gives utterance to some detached precepts, including the compendious rule : ' Whatsoever things are true, or noble, or just, or pure, or lovely, or of good report, think on these things.'

With an abruptness still more remarkable, as show-ing how vividly the thought of them was present to the Apostle's mind, come the few brief commands of which the text is one. Between the intimation that Apollos could not come to them as yet, and the precept to submit themselves to the household of Stephanas their chief native teacher,—perhaps thinking of the dependent craving of some of them for the immediate presence of Apollos or of himself, St. Paul here ex-claims, 'Watch ye, stand fast in the faith, quit you like men, be strong.'

As in numberless other places of the Gospels and Epistles, the language is borrowed from the Old

Testament; where similar words are addressed literally to men preparing for battle, or figuratively, as in the Psalms, to the faithful in their distress, who are encouraged to trust in God's defence against their enemies.

But the enemy against whom the Corinthians are told to stand fast and quit themselves like men, is the spirit of party strife; the strength or courage which they are invited to exercise, is the firmness of an inward determination against evil, not to be swayed by temptation, nor beguiled from the simplicity of Christ.

The exhortation has reference to their special circumstances, in a Church beset by heathen and Jewish enemies, and endangered by half-heathen and half-Jewish members—in peril of being torn to pieces by the emulation of opposing sects, or at another moment of being polluted by the universal allowance of some flagrant sin.

But just as the Apostle has here given a moral and spiritual meaning to an expression of old Jewish patriotism, so we may seek for a still wider application of his words; and, in a different state of the Church and of the world, we may find a universal Christian import in his stirring trumpet-call, 'Quit you like men, be strong.' Of the Christian ideal which is set before us as a rule of life, one element or aspect, perhaps hardly made prominent enough in religious teaching, is moral strength. And yet surely there is no part of holiness that has a more winning power. Men may not at once desire humility or meekness or charity, when they admire them; but there is no man at all conscious of his own weakness, who would not wish to be made strong. Whoever has felt that the courage and firmness and nobleness and, in one word, the strength of the Christian character, as delineated in the New Testament, are quite above the level of ordinary human life, can hardly help longing to be religious. The aspirations awakened by other traits of Christ are more akin to emotion, but none can be more practically operative than this. 'If we talk of strength, lo, He is strong.' To the Christian this is not a cause of discouragement, but of hope. For God in Christ has taught us to make His own perfection the aim of our endeavour, and Christ himself is our support as we press on. And the more we feel the infirmity of our own nature, the more we shall seek to be strengthened by His Spirit in the inner man, by looking to Him in faith, and learning of Him. And so our weakness will become our strength. For this is one of the paradoxes of the religious life, in which so many seeming opposites are harmonized. He who is dead to the world is yet devoted to the world's good: he who sets his face like a flint against all men for the truth's sake, will yet become all things to all men that he may win some: the meekest of men is also the

most courageous; the most humble is the most confident ; he is the last to assert himself and yet the last
to yield.   And thus the image of Christian firmness
is to be sought, not in vehemence and daring im-
petuosity, nor in those qualities which most directly
impress mankind ; but is often found in one outwardly
feeble and encompassed with infirmities, who by
God's help has won the victory over self, and has a
clear eye for duty, and can by no means be turned
aside from the service of God and man.   So various
and complex are the possibilities of human character,
that one who was amongst his contemporaries in
weakness and fear and in much trembling, whose
bodily presence was weak and his speech contemptible, is the great example to after-ages of religious
heroism.

One great secret of all true power is singleness of
aim.   It is so in every path of life.   He is really
successful, amongst professional men, whose first
thought for years together has been the work of his
profession.   If an army or a ship's crew performs, as
we sometimes say, miracles of endurance or bravery,
what is the cause?   Is it not that one thought has
reigned sole in the breast of every man, the thought
of honour, or better still, of duty?   The adventurous
traveller is supported through unheard-of dangers,
privations, and distresses, by the one thought of the
object of his long and perilous toil—whether this be to

discover new lands, or to determine some point in science, or to ameliorate the condition of savage tribes. The same is true of every inventor and discoverer. Sir Isaac Newton, when some one marvelled at the great achievements of his genius, is said to have replied that if he differed at all from other inquirers it was in patience only. In other words, the single object of his life was ever before him and constantly preferred to all things else.

But there is a higher aim than that of any separate calling or profession, although for most men not irreconcileable with the round of ordinary duty. This aim is single ; for goodness and truth are really one, though the full scope and meaning of the high endeavour cannot be crushed into a phrase. It has a religious aspect, 'To do Thy will, O God ;' it has a spiritual aspect, to do nothing against the truth, but for the truth ; it has a moral aspect, to serve and bless mankind. This was the aim for which Christ lived, and for which He died. This is the true life, of which the elements are perfectly united in Him. This is the secret of His victorious strength, of His unconquerable fearlessness, of His divine repose. To do the will of His Father by making known that will ; to withhold no smallest particle of the truth which He had heard of God—the truth that God is love, the will of God that men should in reality become the children of God ; to extend to all men everywhere in

His own person, by act and word, the lovingkindness and righteousness of the Almighty Father: this, if we may say it reverently, was the motive of His divine life. For this He was in hunger and weariness, and knew not where to lay His head; for this He spent His nights upon the mountain side, and went about with the twelve preaching and healing everywhere; for this He bore with their ignorance and unbelief; for this He drew upon Himself the hatred and envy of the ruling class amongst His countrymen, and calmly faced them even to death. Words cannot utter the depth and beauty of that life; but not less wondrous than the depth and beauty is the Godlike strength which, in poverty, and apparent failure, and desertion, and betrayal, overcame the world—which the flattery of affection, the soothing voice of friendship, and the sophistry of designing enemies, were equally powerless to hinder or to ensnare.

Let us now turn from this exalted pattern to the 'low level' of our common existence, and instance some of the many ways in which we seem to need some portion of the strength that was in Christ, of the manfulness which St. Paul enjoins. We have need of this in personal character, in society, in religion.

First, in the individual life there is the weakness of self-indulgence, the weakness of indolence, the weakness of giving way to habit. There are the infirmities of vanity, and caprice, and levity, which take so much from the grace and harmony of our being. Had we only more continually before us even an imperfect ideal of what man ought to be, should we not many a time be up and doing, when, as it is, we live a burden to the ground? And would not many a weak place in every life be healed?

That patience is allied to strength we may be reminded by the striking verse of the Psalms, 'God is a righteous judge, strong and patient, and God is provoked every day.' But if we always remembered that impatience is a sign of weakness, that forbearance is an attribute of power, should we so often yield to the illusion, which makes us think that we are exerting strength, when we have lost that true strength and firmness which is inseparable from calm? Another form of strength is a faithful spirit. Unfaithfulness is the penalty of a weak and shallow nature. The triumph of affection is not the blaze of passion, but to be long tried and true. The evils which beset us severally may, in short, for the most part, be referred to the want of self-control. And to be self-controlled is individually to be strong.

Are there not still more obvious weaknesses in our social life? Would it not almost seem at times as if individuality was lost in the mere habit of society? And if this were altogether a community of human kindness, all were so far well: but does not the same fountain send forth sweet waters and bitter? Are not tales, whether good or bad, apt to be repeated and circulated with the same want of thought? Does the force of example depend alto-gether upon its excellence, or that of a custom on its reasonableness and propriety? Can it be said that our social code has any much higher rule than that of 'doing as others do;' unless, indeed, there be sometimes a rule opposed to this, of 'doing as we please'? But if each had before him as a sacred end the good of all, the furtherance of truth and right—that is, in Scripture language, the kingdom of God—how much more life and meaning would be imparted to our common daily intercourse, how many an evil tendency that has sprung up unsuspected, while men slept, would be swept away by the force of higher interests!

Too often, as one writes, 'the greater part can only detect the evil when it comes forth from them, nearly as when any other might observe it.' But to look around with thoughtful observation, not without cha-rity, may help us in the more difficult task of looking within. And it were often well for us if we had eyes to see our failings, written as it were in large charac-ters, in those blots upon the national life, about which to a reasonable mind there can be no mistake.

Now amongst social infirmities there may be in-stanced, as one of the most insidious, the tendency to class prejudices. In proportion to the force of

humanity in man is the feeling of universal brotherhood, the power of sympathizing with all conditions.
That we should ever encourage one another in valuing
or dispraising men, not according to their real worth,
but as they stand related to our class, to our profession, to our school or academy, to our *set* in society,
is surely a signal instance of weakness. That we
should be even involuntarily affected by such an infirmity is a misfortune. We are told by the father
of history that the Medes of the 5th century B. C.,
even after the empire had departed from them,
'were accustomed to honour most of all men those
living nearest to themselves (their own selves only
excepted); and in the next degree those once removed in place; and so on in like manner, having
in least respect those who dwelt farthest off: believing,' he continues, 'that they themselves are by
far the best of all men, and that the rest lay claim
to goodness in the ratio aforesaid, and that those who
live most remote from them are the worst.' Are we
much more rational often in our judgments of men?

There are times when all goes smoothly whether
we are strong or weak; but there are other times
when it is of deep consequence what spirit we
are of. In reverses of fortune, in bereavement, in the
sick chamber, in the face of death, we all need a
strength and a support that rests somewhere beyond
the storms of the world. Whether the effect of sorrow

is to ennoble or to depress, to harden or to enlarge
the heart, whether in times of extreme trial we are
disgraced in our own eyes, or quit ourselves valiantly,
must greatly depend on the spirit in which we have
sought to live all along. It is true that latent strength
is often called forth by circumstances, that power is
given, as we say, where it is needed : but who can tell
in such cases what preparations of the heart have
gone before, what aspirations of past years, what
forgotten resolutions, are re-awakened in the presence
of the great opportunity or the crushing blow? To
speak generally, the foundation of this strength is
laid in early life, when every temptation mastered
is a source of future power, when to have a fixed
purpose and to pursue it steadfastly, to sacrifice present ease to coming good, nerves the whole man for
a still higher endeavour. And even if performance
come far short of resolve, let the young still place their
standard high. Let them not lose faith in the sun-clad
power of goodness, purity, and truth, nor cease to
follow these, because they find that action lags behind
the flight of purpose. There is also a peculiar strength
that should accompany old age. There are those
who, even in much bodily infirmity, never sink into
a mere routine of unconscious habit, whose eye, that
looks back calmly over a chequered course, and has
gathered wisdom from various fortunes, looks also
with kindly sagacious interest on the fortunes and

the work of others. Such an one by a quiet word, spoken, it may be, in a sick room, will sometimes effect more than can be wrought by oratory.

And there are some who, in the even tenour of the years between youth and age, when the time of illusions is passed, and the career is fixed, and the game of ambition is played out, instead of yielding to vain regrets over losses and perhaps errors that are irreparable, are seen to cling with unabating energy to the sphere in which their lot is finally cast, and to work nobly on, with no hope of earthly recompense, at the humble duties which are still given them to do.

In the last place it remains to notice one more particular in which the injunction of the Apostle is to be obeyed. If we are right in thinking that religion is strength, what are we to think of weakness in religion? By what other name shall we characterize some of the so-called religious impulses of our day? If sentimental effusion takes the place of strenuous honest purpose; if more is thought of modes of symbolism or of sensible impression than of the rule of life; if beliefs which our forefathers solemnly rejected are embraced by a superstitious fancy, without any serious inquiry whether they be true, what becomes of Christianity as the religion pre-eminently of righteousness and truth? He who has once become careless about what is true in matters of religion, however trying may be the problem in our day, has yielded up the citadel of his mind. He cannot tell what strange delusion may take possession of him.

The question after all returns, 'Who is sufficient for these things?' And we still answer with St. Paul, 'Our sufficiency is of God.' He is not far from those who diligently seek Him. We rest also on the support of Christ, who, 'when we were without strength,' gave Himself to raise mankind from sin to holiness.

To believe firmly in the sacredness of truth and the eternity of right—that is of itself a mighty anchor of the soul : there have been noble spirits that have manfully ridden out the storm on this alone. To believe in the Eternal Father, who is infinitely righteous and true, whose all-embracing love is ever ready to awaken the better self which He has implanted in us and all men, who has provided for the completion hereafter of that work of righteousness which He has partially revealed on earth—this is surely a strong motive to live strenuously in the hope of being made instruments of that work. And to believe in Christ, the Christ of the Gospels, who has awakened in man this deeper consciousness of God, who has opened the way for him to a life of blessedness above all that the human heart without Him had conceived, whose image, as reflected for us in those simple records, far exceeds in beauty and sublimity the fond

imaginations of a later time, who communicates
to us that unchanging love which ministers comfort to the penitent, and hope to the despairing
soul—that is a stay to which all, however feeble
and weary, may boldly cling. 'He giveth power
to the faint, and to them that have no might He
increaseth strength.'

M

SERMON XIII.

THE FRUIT OF LABOUR.

1869.

'For to me to live is Christ, and to die is gain. But if I live in the flesh, this is the fruit of my labour: yet what I shall choose I wot not. For I am in a strait betwixt two, having a desire to depart, and to be with Christ; which is far better. Nevertheless to abide in the flesh is more needful for you.'—PHILIPPIANS i. 21–24.

THESE familiar words are the expression of a mode of feeling, which is above and beyond the range of common human experience. They are the utterance of an extraordinary person in an extraordinary time, of St. Paul in the last stage of his career—an utterance higher than any we could dare to make, perhaps also somewhat different in kind. And yet they are full of instruction to us and all men, and the lesson that they teach is very simple and practical.

We should indeed gain comparatively little by trying to appropriate the language of such passages immediately to ourselves, and so to conjure into transient life an imitative glow of feeling. Such attempts may be not unnatural in some early phases

of religion, when to the newly awakened heart all
seems alike that bears the mark of piety, and every
flight seems possible to the aspiring soul. Many have
so received their first impressions of the truth. But
when persevered in, this crude and unenlightened use
of Scripture language has two defects. It is apt to
be associated with a mere effusion of feeling, which
may weaken instead of regulating the real springs of
action : and, however valuable it may have proved to
some, it has the effect of deadening the words of
Scripture, and robbing them of their true life and
power for many others; so that it is only by an effort
that we can dissociate them from their hackneyed use,
only by breaking through the petrifying crust of years
that we can approach the living fountain. It is
otherwise that we shall seek to profit by the examples that are set before us in the Bible, if we are
rational men. We shall feel the incongruity of
taking directly to ourselves the language of an
Apostle—we, who are not in cold, or nakedness, or
in bonds for the Gospel's sake, nor in hunger and
thirst, nor watchings, nor perils by land and sea,
nor burdened with the care of all the churches—
we who at most are striving, amidst a dangerous
excess of comforts, to do in a narrow spot of earth
some daily portion of that which it is our duty to
do. But for the very reason that we cannot adopt
his language, and only very imperfectly breathe his

spirit, it is good for us to remember that such a
man as St. Paul once lived and moved upon this
earth, where we also have to live and die. It is
good to remember that these words ónce came from
the fulness of a living heart, not uttered in a formal
prayer or sermon, when the man was expected to say
what should be elevating or impressive, but in the
unrestrained intercourse of friendship, in a letter
which breathes the warmth and tenderness of con-
fiding affection, and which was written by way of
acknowledgment for a timely gift.

On an occasion so apparently slight, he whose heart
was ever on his lips in holding communion with those
to whom he had taught the gospel, wrote, according
to a slightly different rendering: 'To me to live is
Christ, and to die is gain. But seeing that to live
on in the flesh is to me the fruit of labour, I know
not which to choose. For I am straitened between
the two, my desire being to depart and be with
Christ, for that is far better; but to abide still in
the flesh is more needful for your sakes.'

Such words can never lose their power. They
come down to us from a purer air; yet the voice
is human, and is audible to all who feel. They
sum up the constant tenour of a life, which, like all
great lives, is able at once to shame us and to
inspire, and also to teach a lesson which may be

applied to the most various conditions of human existence.

I. Let us try to think of the fact which the words imply. There was once a man who, longing, as for hid treasure, not for death but for the joy beyond, yet chose to live—not for life's sake, for he knew that more and fuller life awaited him—not for the comforts of home, he was a solitary in bonds and amongst enemies, and even with friends deserting him ('Thou knowest that all they of Asia have turned away')— not for the enjoyment of riches, for he was dependent and poor—not in the hope of supplanting others by fair or crooked means, and 'getting on,' as we phrase it, 'in society;' the freedmen of Cæsar's household probably thought themselves princes as compared with him—but simply that he might abound in labours and in sufferings for the truth, and for those weaker than himself, who still needed to be strengthened and supported by him. And whether in life or death, his thoughts all centred for their sole object in Christ, the source of this wondrous life, to whom death would only bring him nearer. Think of all this, and then think of the petty rivalries, the mean pleasures, the waste of power, the frivolous talk, the ungenerous feeling, the mean policy, the mere idle vacancy, which beset our common life; and, however little we may hope to pass at once from this to that, we cannot but feel the weight of the rebuke. Can we realize, have we ever sought to realize, the certainty of our own death?   How then shall we compare our lives to his, who looked with open face beyond the grave, desiring to depart, and yet for the sake of others was content to live,

> 'To absent him from felicity awhile,
> And in this harsh world draw his breath with pain'?

Yet, on further reflection, it does not seem so impossible that we, in an altered state both of the Church and world, may receive something of the spirit that was in Paul.   His example may animate rather than discourage us.   We too, in our low degree, may learn as Christians to look steadily in the face of death : and we may learn more and more to live as seeing Him who is invisible.   We shall learn both these things just in proportion as we have also learnt to live for others, and to work for them as in the sight of God.   Times and circumstances alter, the characters of men are diverse ; but the elements of the Christian life remain the same.   Nor are we wholly without patterns, even in these days, of Christian virtue and nobleness, on which it is good for us to dwell—not reaching, it may be, to the ideal height or the heroic stature, but all the more affecting and instructive because breathing the same air with us, and though ofttimes compassed with infirmity, having yet 'a glory portioned in the scale.'

There must be many who, at some time or other of their lives, have had the opportunity of watching the motions of a character who seemed to be lifted above the earth, of one who was ready to give up all worldly interests for a cause of truth or right, who would make any sacrifice where there was hope of doing good, or in whom affection for kindred or friends had literally burned up every selfish consideration. Amongst those whom it has been our lot to reverence in this world, some may have had more of intellectual insight, others more of practical energy, they may have had more or less of natural reserve, and more or less of fervour and enthusiasm; but in the determination to do good as they had opportunity, and at all costs to be faithful and true, in the princely heart of innocence, in the simplicity of noble and unselfish purpose, do we not recognize in all a common type of spiritual strength, in which they resemble the great and good of old?

Or if some have been less fortunate, either from the dearth of such high examples, or the want of an eye to see them, let them turn to the biographies of good men, and they will find abundant proof that in no age has God left Himself without a witness to that pure and undefiled religion, whose elevating influence is ever most felt when speaking through a life. Few things are more refreshing, especially when we are tempted to despair of the possibility of goodness in ourselves or in the world around us, than to take up such a book, for instance, as the Memoir of Richard Baxter, and trace the increasing power of Christianity in an honest heart.

It is true that men are often withheld from seeing the goodness that is passing before their eyes. They recognize the popular qualities; but the popular qualities are not the highest. We are apt to measure the amount of love and labour which is spent in our behalf by the degree of compliance to our own opinion and feeling, with which the work of self-devotion is accompanied. But when that which has opposed us is taken out of the way, when the jar of earthly interests can no longer ruffle the surface of the heart, then every generous mind will see the good revealed, and will acknowledge the excellence of that disinterested endeavour which is emphatically ‘ not of this world.’

II. We turn now to the general lesson which may be drawn from the text ; to what in modern language may be called the leading idea contained in it.

For every record of true greatness is profitable, not only for reproof and correction, but also for doctrine and instruction in righteousness. Christianity, for instance, is not fully taught by merely pointing to the man Christ Jesus, to His acts and sufferings. The principles of that life may be as simple as they are deep; but as they are of lasting import, so they are capable of expression. And so, if we would learn all we can from St. Paul, we must think of his words until we find in them a universal truth, as applicable to our times as to his. And the truth which may be gathered from these words is something of this kind. The Christian ideal of blessedness has two aspects, which both meet in Christ: one inward and upward, looking towards communion with God; and one outward and around, looking towards our brethren of mankind, especially towards the weaker brethren— those little ones for whom Christ died.

It is often asserted in the present day, and what is often asserted is apt to be temporarily believed, that Christianity tends only upwards: that it is the effect of our religion to direct men's gaze into a distant and unknown heaven, while the realities of life pass by them unregarded: that Christians are absorbed in 'theological and metaphysical controversies,' to the neglect of social well-being: that the thought of the invisible future has swallowed up the visible present, and that we relinquish the substance of this life for the shadow of another. We can only answer that in so far as this has been so, we have been untrue to the spirit of our own sacred books. There may be some sting in the taunt, as directed against historical Christianity, in which the intention of the Divine Founder has been only partially realized. It is with mixed feelings that we look back upon the asceticism of the Middle Ages, or on the Crusades, or again on the theology of the seventeenth century, or even on the religious movements of sixty years since. We must not refuse to learn even from professed enemies, who show us where in our spiritual warfare we are beating the air; though we may have to acknowledge that, could we but have seen to read it, the lesson was already written for us in the plainest terms. We may plead perhaps that no lesson is learnt all at once, least of all a lesson so deep and wide as the meaning of the life of Christ: and that in the history of all ideas some vague aspiration has ever preceded the final practical effect. But to show that Christianity has a blessing for the life that now is, as well as for the life to come, we need go no further than the Epistles of St. Paul. In detail we are not called upon to copy him, although in every detail there is a sagacity, and moderation, and tact, mingled with his enthusiasm, which give the example of a worldly prudence wiser than the wisdom of this world. But where has the general principle of 'living for others' ever been so nobly exemplified? Where shall we find such solicitous and tender care for the true well-being of others here in time, as well as for their ultimate perfection? Or who can accuse St. Paul of caring selfishly for his own salvation, as if that were the goal of his endeavour, when, in his eagerness to bring his own nation to the truth, he expresses himself as willing to be accurst from Christ;

when, knowing that to depart and be with Christ is
far better, he yet prayed that he might live to give
strength to struggling churches; when, with the end
in view, and the crown of glory certain in his eye, he
could not think of his own reward apart from his
brethren : 'A crown of glory which the Lord, the
righteous Judge, shall give me in that day, *and not to
me only, but to all those that love His appearing.*'

To act in the present, to live for others, to redeem
the time, to use all means for bettering the physical
and social, as well as the moral and spiritual condition
of mankind—these, it need hardly be said to a
Christian audience, are precepts in full accordance
with Christianity. But the thought of another life,
for which this is the seedtime and preparation, in
which some obstacles that check the flow of goodness
here will be removed, and whatever we have sown of
righteousness will bear fruit a thousandfold—this,
instead of being out of harmony with such duties, is
the greatest of all incentives to them. For if we lay
to heart the words, 'Inasmuch as ye did it unto the
least of these my brethren, ye did it unto me,' we
shall learn that life in Christ is not separable from life
in duty; that if the soul is permitted to retire inwards
for communion with God, this is only in order that in
the strength of such food she may go forth to action
with greater power; that we cannot say 'Our Father,'
without adding 'Thy will be done in earth;' that

every grace of God, like the seven loaves of the miracle, is increased through being imparted ; and that the hope of heaven cannot exist apart from the hope that life on earth may be the 'fruit of labour.'

For our belief of immortality is dependent on our belief in God ; and, as we are moral beings, our belief in God grows strong or weak with our belief in the supremacy of good. But if all souls are God's, who will do with all that which is just and right, what notion can we form of eternal life but that of partaking of the divine nature, through becoming conscious instruments of His good and righteous will towards men ? That is the good work which He begins in us here, and which gives us confidence that He will perform it to the end : a work not of selfish isolation, but of communion and fellowship with all—with those likeminded with us, that we may have some interchange of grace —with those from whom we differ, that we may find the points of agreement between us more important than those in which we differ ;— communion with those more advanced than we are, that we may receive some gift ; and with those still faltering at the entrance of the way, that we may win the higher blessedness of strengthening them.

Will that communion and fellowship be less binding, will the religious motive to labour for mankind be less constraining, because we know that this life is not all, 'that all we see is but an endless work begun'? Surely far otherwise. That men without such an inspiring hope should be found to labour for mankind, is indeed a strong proof of zeal—a zeal which one would think must, even if unconsciously, have some higher end than to raise man a little above the brutes. But how much more earnestly ought those to labour, who have been taught the infinite worth of every human spirit, to whom every moment of time includes possibilities of eternal value, and who, in working for others in the cause of truth and right, believe that they are fellow-workers with the Almighty!

The widening of our earthly horizons in the later ages, through the revelations of science, may naturally for a moment rivet our gaze earthwards. But only for a moment. Our second thought should be one of thankfulness, that there has been given to us a larger measure of that which we can never fully comprehend, the knowledge of the work which God worketh from the beginning to the end : that there have been given us richer means of usefulness, and untold powers for good.

But as in our thankfulness we look upwards, do we see a corresponding enlargement of the heavenly horizons? The answer is more doubtful. Some mists of error have been dispelled; some dark clouds that rested even on the highest intellects of former days have passed or are slowly passing away: but such negative gains, though doubtless blessed for the race, will be of small effect for us, if we practically lose hold of the central truth, that goodness is divine and eternal. Let theology be purified as it may, no theory can surpass the reality of the life of Christ; no enlightenment can be a substitute for that prophetic fire, which Moses prayed that all the people might receive, which Milton prematurely boasted that they had received, which comes forth from the growing consciousness of a present God, of His goodwill to men, and of the powers of the life to come.

If our heart is fixed in the belief that God is good and true, and if we cling to this against all appearances and through all trials, and if we strive continually to realize this belief in act, we shall not be dismayed at the thought of our own death, nor shall we be vexed with anxiety for those whom God takes away from us to Himself. There are sadder things than death in this world. But there is one desire which the thought of death should quicken in us all, and that is, that our life, while it lasts, may be the fruit of labour.

SERMON XIV.

'The days will come, when ye shall desire to see one of the days of the Son of man.'—LUKE xvii. 22.

'And now abideth faith, hope, charity, these three; but the greatest of these is charity.'—1 COR. xiii. 13.

CHRISTIANITY may be regarded personally or impersonally, as the following of Christ or as the realization of a divine ideal. There are some who find their chief support in thinking of the Saviour himself, while some would dwell rather on the spirit of His teaching. To the heart of many Christians He is more than His words, and more than any lesson to be drawn from His life. To the mind of others the eternal truth which He revealed and the principles of His divine life appear to have their full value only when they are considered absolutely, and as having a meaning which is independent of history. Neither aspect is complete without the other. Mere feeling may hold principles in solution, as it were, but is imperfectly conscious of them, and is apt to lose something either of clearness or of breadth, becoming either intense and narrow, or diffusive and vague ; and the attempt of the intellect to separate ideas from their origin, and to view them abstractedly in themselves, may, if pursued exclusively, tend to weaken character.

I propose, first, to speak of Jesus Christ as one who has called us friends ; and secondly, of faith and hope and love, as exemplified in Him, and as first principles or essential elements of the Christian life.

1. Jesus is our Friend, because He was the Friend of all men ; because we feel that there were no limits to His human and divine love. He whose compassion went forth effectually to thousands in a single day; He who sat down to eat with publicans and sinners at the invitation of one of them whom He had called; who accepted the humble penitent ; who, having once loved any, loved them unto the end ; He who stretched forth His hands to His disciples, and said, ' Behold my mother and my brethren,'—has a heart that can embrace all men. When we read of His giving Himself for men, we feel that though we have not seen Him we have been the objects of His love, and that we are receivers of the gifts which He died bestowing. We cannot think ourselves excluded, unless we are of those who keep back the truth or hinder the work of goodness ; and in so far as any are or have been so, the very fierceness of His rebuke, ' Woe unto you

that shut up the kingdom of heaven against men,' may convince us alike of His love to souls, and of our need of partaking in His spirit.

2. He is our Friend, because He convinces us of sin. In straining our gaze backward through time, beyond the ideal of the Reformers, beyond the ideal of the mediæval mystic, even beyond the ideal of the early Church, and in trying to see Him as He really was in Galilee and Jerusalem, the eye will sometimes swim in mists of uncertainty. But we see enough to know that the worship of eighteen centuries has not been an error, and that all other lives are partial when compared with His. Whatever may be our own nature and circumstances, we cannot draw near to that image of perfect purity, tenderness, and strength, of absolute fearlessness in the assertion of truth, of absolute devotedness to the eternal good of men, without being made aware that in some way we have fallen short of what God would have us to be, of that which we ourselves desire to be. What need of enumerating the blots which become manifest, even in holy lives, when shorn of false hues through this correcting glass? Impatience, timidity, extravagance, indolence, the prevalence of one idea, personal respects, the blindness of affection, inconsiderate judgment, limitations and narrowness of all kinds, the faults of weakness, the faults of unchastened strength ; all these are continually showing that we have an

imperfect hold of the will of God and of the good
of man.   Christ ever held to both with a tenacity of
love which no power could ever in the least unfasten.
And therefore He at once rebukes and animates
us.   All high examples do this in their degree;
but in Jesus Christ the power of conviction and of
encouragement is inexhaustible.   In any separate part
of life, as in an art which we are learning, or an
endeavour on which the future hangs, we are grateful
soon or late to one who only shows us our defects.
But he who shows us where we fail, and in the same act,
by example, or teaching, or sympathy, or some hidden
power, enables us to do better afterwards, is the one
who immediately and irresistibly wins our gratitude.
And this is what Christ does for us in the whole of life.

3. For, in the third place, He is our Friend because,
while He convinces us of sin, He gives to us the
power of faith in God.   The fact that such a life
was lived upon the earth, makes easier for men till
the end of time the practical belief in One above
'from whom all goodness flows.'   And this faith becomes still clearer when we find that Jesus himself
referred the secret of His strength to His union with
One whom He called His Father in heaven.   As we
draw nearer to Him with love, we 'believe in His
belief;' and it is a belief in which there is no offence.
Whatever intellectual difficulties may arise from facts
of experience or from peculiarities of mental history,

the God whom Christ revealed will ever be acceptable to the moral nature and to the heart of man. The loving Father of all His children, who is kind even to the unthankful and to the evil, who goes forth to meet the penitent from afar off, and to save men from their sins will give even His beloved Son ; a God who judges by no arbitrary or traditional standard, but by the law of love, and judges only that He may save ; a God of perfect righteousness, whose will is that all His creatures shall partake of His righteousness and become holy, as He is holy—this thought of our unseen Father, who will forgive our debts as we forgive our debtors, can never cease to win the spiritual affections of mankind. And when this thought has become a practical principle, firmly fixed within and going forth continually in action, then the assurance of faith is realized.

4. Fourthly, Jesus is our Friend because He gives us also the assurance of hope. In His life we have the earnest of a regenerated humanity. If the love of Christ has given us a light of faith which shines upon our own individual path, His Spirit also sheds a light of hope upon the darkness of this world. On first awakening from some ideal vision of perfection and peace, which aspiration has painted on the heaven of our inward sight, we may be startled by the harsh realities that crowd in upon us, until we remember Him who, foreseeing the end from the

beginning, sent forth His twelve apostles on their desperate mission, preached the coming of the kingdom when He knew not where to lay His head, and, in the parables of the grain of mustard seed and of the leaven, calmly affirmed that the spread of truth and righteousness would be slow and gradual, but ultimately universal.

We cannot despair of the world of which He did not despair ; we have gentler thoughts of that human nature which He claimed as the Son of Man ; we know that truth and right are the greatest powers in the universe, and must prevail.

In a word, then, we have such a Friend, who has loved us even before our birth with an all-embracing love, a love purer and therefore stronger than that of others. And His desire in dying was that we should be saved from all that is base, and mean, and unlovely, and untrue, and wrong, and that we should rise and follow Him in the path of righteousness, and become partakers of the blessed life. Is it any reason for our frustrating that desire, for remaining contented with a low and perverse condition of soul, for being indifferent to all higher aims, that our Friend is absent, and that, although we know what great things He has done for us, we have never seen Him ? Or rather, is it not when He is removed from sight that the sayings of our Friend sink down into the heart, and we begin to recognize their essential value?

This leads us to the second part of our subject. For this personal ground of the obligation to Christian obedience is not the only ground, though I have dwelt long upon it, because it naturally commends itself to so many. Jesus would have us listen to His words, not merely because they are His, but because they are true. If He were now on earth He might recall many of us from speculations about His person to the practical fulfilment of His teaching. 'Why call ye me Lord, Lord, and do not the things that I say?' If we would keep the feast of His nativity as He would wish us to do, we must keep it as the birthday of Christianity, and of the kingdom of God and righteousness upon the earth. We hold Him as divine, not only because we have been taught so, but because in those few broken years of His ministry He founded the divine religion whose essential truth we believe to be eternal, and whose universal acceptance, so far as that essential truth is concerned, we regard as only a question of time. The spirit of Christianity is the meaning of the life of Christ; and that meaning is summed up in St. Paul's words: 'Now abideth faith, hope, love, these three; but the greatest of these is love.' These are the permanent elements of our religion, whose force is to remain, when tongues

have ceased, and prophecy fails, and human knowledge of things divine seems to be vanishing away.

Faith, not looking backwards, but forwards, over-
coming the present by realizing what is future and
unseen; not scorning experience, but seeking ever
to learn the application of true principles through
the light of facts.   A faith that has the courage of
its own convictions, because its vision is direct and
practical ; which sees clearly because it has a single
aim, which sees far because it soars so high.   A calm
faith, which can afford to wait, because it is so certain
of the ultimate triumph of good; an earnest faith,
which cannot rest inactive, but must work on perse-
veringly, though with little immediate result.   A faith
not for ourselves alone, but for the world, and especially for all who have been brought within our
sphere ; trusting them to the Almighty purposes, but
ever roused anew to labour for them, as being fellow-
workers with God.   Faith in God and in His goodwill towards men.   Faith in that nature which was
made in the image of God.   Faith in the victory of
justice, mercy, and truth.   Faith in the power of
enlightened self-devotion to renew mankind.   Such
is the abiding principle of Christian faith.

And Christian hope is like unto it, if it be not
rather the very bloom and exuberance of Christian
faith.   Hope, not of any outward good, but of endless

progress in partaking of the life of God. Hope, not of any special changes in one spot of earth, but of the spiritual improvement of the race, to be effected both from without and from within. A hope that is not easily cast down, but, as guided by faith and not by sight, is brightest in the darkest gloom, like the hope which noble Frenchmen have been lately cherishing, of the regeneration of their country. A hope that by its inherent life bursts the bands of fatalism, and cannot be held down with reflections on the degeneracy of the age, or the inveteracy of inherited defect, but can estimate the possibilities of moral growth.

> ' It is an ever-fixed mark,
> Which looks on tempests, but is never shaken;
> It is the star to every wandering bark,
> Whose worth 's unknown, although his height be taken.'

Nor can this hope be satisfied with the conviction, to which it still must cling, that in the after life that is unknown to us, every soul of man will receive the just and merciful award :—

> ' That good shall fall,
> At last—far off—at last, to all.'

For such an anticipation of things beyond our reach, although comforting, is all too consistent with feeble and languid efforts for the actual good of men. And Christian hope is active, full of energy; it is the life of Christian work, that is, of all work that is worth the doing. The Christian life knows not despair ; it possesses the soul in patience, it watches unweariedly for the good of others. Like an eastward mountain summit, it is flushed with radiance when all things far and near are still wrapt in night.

Faith is the strong stem of the tree, which puts forth the leaves and blossoms of hope ; but love is the root, which ministers life and sap to all other graces of the soul. It is love that believeth all things ; it is love that hopeth all things. This is the secret of the life which Christian fancy delights to think of as beginning on this day, in ' the light that shone when hope was born.' And Christian love, too, is no mere sentiment, but an active principle, working in the lives of Christians according to their measure, as it wrought without measure in the life of Christ. It is not only the communion of the brethren ; for Christ Himself has said, and His words remain as a warning to His followers, ' If ye salute your brethren only, what do ye more than others ? ' Nor is it only the ' enthusiasm of humanity,' claiming brotherhood with all that wear the form of man. It is this. and more than this ; the intense desire, or rather the determination, to extend the blessings of truth and goodness to all that come within our reach. No blind passionate longing, no weak craving for sympathy; but the simple continued act of giving more than we receive.

This love is fearless and direct, because it is so strong; it has no reserves, no suspicion of being misunderstood. It goes ever forth and ever onward, withholding no good from any, freely extending help according as there is opportunity and according as there is any need. To apply a fine saying of an Indian sage, ' It moves not only with but against the wind.' Such is the love that 'seeketh not her own, is not easily provoked, thinketh no evil, rejoiceth not in iniquity, but rejoiceth in the truth.' Other affections are limited, perhaps exclusive, in proportion to their intensity: this extends more widely as it becomes more vivid in central energy.

In conclusion, we may return once more to the personal side of our religion. For the virtues of which the Apostle speaks are no mere abstract names to us; we have seen them livingly exemplified in those whose hands we have clasped in ours, whose looks and tones and gestures we remember well.

The saintly one, who seemed to borrow an unearthly grace as the outward form decayed, who spoke quite simply of an ever-strengthening trust that was confirmed by sorrow, who, dwelling amongst the lesser things of life and ever mindful of the least of them, was in all this only striving with painful effort to make life more beautiful—such an one shall be the image to us of the faith in things unseen.

Some strong heroic soul, earnest and blithe, that having descried a world of good unrealized, went on with quenchless ardour over rough and smooth, till all around had caught the irresistible fire—shall still cheer us onwards as with the voice of hope.

And some one, who in a few short years did the work of many a lifetime, whose ever-joyous spirit was most gladdened when he could help a friend, whose loyalty to those once loved by him was only exceeded by his free, spontaneous activity in labouring for the general good—shall forbid us to confuse or to degrade the type of manly Christian love.

Such there have been, and our eyes have seen them. They rest from earthly labour: our work is before us still. Let us likewise seek to be strong in faith, patient through hope, and rooted in charity; that, even amidst 'the waves of this troublesome world,' we may be members with them of that unbroken communion of the saints, one family in earth and heaven, of which Christ is the Head and Lord; while all that is lovely and of good report, all that ministers to the higher good of man, whether owning Him or not, has a place in the fellowship of His kingdom.

SERMON XV.

ON PRAYER.

1863.

'Your Father knoweth what things ye have need of, before ye ask Him.'—MATT. vi. 8.

THESE words of Christ are introductory to the example which He gave to His disciples of the manner in which they ought to pray; and they afford the reason of the precept, 'When ye pray, use not vain repetitions,' or unmeaning phrases, 'as the heathen do;' (with which may be compared the words of the Hebrew preacher: 'Be not rash with thy mouth, and let not thy heart be hasty to utter anything before God: for He is in heaven and thou upon earth, therefore let thy words be few'). 'They think that they shall be heard for their much speaking. Be not like unto them; for your Father knoweth what things ye have need of, before ye ask Him.'

This is one of those sayings of our Lord, which not only go directly to the heart of every man, but also by their simple utterance convince the reason; such as are these also from the same Sermon on the mount: 'He maketh His sun to rise on the evil and on the good.' 'Where your treasure is, there will your heart be also.' 'No man can serve two masters.' 'Which of you by taking thought can add a cubit to his stature?' 'Whatsoever ye would that men should do to you, even so do unto them.'

God, who made all, knows and cares for all. The very hairs of every head are numbered. He is working all together for the final good of all. The unconscious infant, the wild, thoughtless youth, the ripening Christian, lie equally in the full sunshine of His eye, and are borne and carried in the arms of His goodness, which is over all His works, for He is kind even to the unthankful and the evil. Still deeper fountains of His love are opened to those who can receive His love—to those who by patient continuance in well-doing seek for glory, honour, and immortality— to those who are labouring to strengthen others—to those who speak the truth which they have heard from Him. Once more, His love goes forth to the repentant sinner, embracing him while yet a great way off from his Father's home ; not contending against him with great power, but putting strength in him, else the spirit should fail before Him, and the soul which He hath made. In all these ways the love of God is shown anticipating our love, 'Not that we loved Him, but that He first loved us ;' His thought anticipating our thought, 'For there is not a thought in my heart, but lo, O Lord, thou knowest it altogether.'

This consideration of the all-embracing love and care of our heavenly Father is here applied by Jesus Christ himself to modify the natural or first ideas of men respecting *prayer:* 'When ye pray, ye shall not be as the Pharisees are;' and, 'Use not vain repetitions, as the heathen do.'

The earliest prayers arose chiefly from two feelings incident to human nature : the feeling of want and dependence, and the feeling of sin. Like other deep feelings, these were chiefly called forth by temporal calamity, or on occasions of unusual danger, anxiety, or difficulty: 'When He smote them, then they sought Him, and turned them early, and enquired after God.' At such times, though not knowing God, men felt after Him, a power above them, of whom, in the darkness of their ignorance, they dimly guessed. They sought to avert His anger, to propitiate His special favour, to obtain the removal of some distress, or the success of some public or private enterprise. Such were the first upliftings of the human heart to the Almighty; from whence may partly be understood the strange phenomenon, that amongst many primitive and savage peoples the Supreme Being is only known or worshipped as the author of evil. Nor can we doubt that these feeble and erring cries were heard by God, nor that in the course of His providence

they became the source of higher blessings than those
for which the 'praying hands' were (often vainly)
raised. For they contained the germ of those deep
cravings of the human spirit after the Divine, which
found full and final satisfaction in the revelation of
Christ.

The first and simplest prayer, then, is the expression
of spontaneous, natural desire, in the form of a request
to God. Men ask help from one who is mightier than
they are; and in doing so they show their belief that
He is, and their trust, however dimly felt, that He is
the rewarder of those that seek Him. But there is a
question that must sooner or later rise, viz. What
desires are fit to be thus consecrated? And the
answer must depend on men's conception of the
nature and will of Him to whom they pray. No
sane and reverent mind will consciously pray for that
which he knows it to be against God's nature
to grant. For example, no Christian who has been
taught to love his enemies can deliberately pray
to God, who as he has been told is love, for the
fulfilment of a malicious or revengeful wish. The
very thought of bringing such desires into His presence, is enough to rebuke the soul for having har-
boured them. Nor can one who has truly learnt that
God is no respecter of persons, pray consciously for a
blessing on himself which involves the diminution of
the happiness of others. Thus with every step in

our knowledge of God, there is a corresponding eleva-
tion and enlargement of the spirit of prayer. We
know not what things to pray for as we ought, but
there is a Spirit which helpeth our infirmities ; and as
we enter into the communion of that Spirit, our
prayers become more acceptable, because more
spiritual.

I desire in all reverence, endeavouring to follow the
simple meaning of our Lord's own words, to set forth
in brief outline one or two reflections which may help
to clear a subject on which, from the silence often
held regarding it, there exists a good deal of confusion
of thought.

And first, considering prayer merely under the first
or natural form of a petition or request to God,
we are met at once by the limitation spoken of by the
Apostle St. John, 'We know that if we ask anything
according to His will, He heareth us.' So St. Paul
also, in speaking of the prevailing intercession of
the Spirit, says 'He maketh intercession for the saints
according to the will of God.' And we have the
example of Christ himself, who in His extreme agony,
when praying to His Father that the cup of bitterness
might be taken from Him, adds, ' Nevertheless, not
my will, but Thine be done.' 'Thy will be done,' it
has been quaintly said, ' salveth all ; so that whatsoever happens, it is but what our daily prayers
desire.' Let us look also at a negative or opposite

example, which we may find amongst the narratives
of the Old Testament. The prayer of Elijah on two
occasions is referred to by St. James to show that 'the
effectual fervent prayer of a righteous man availeth
much.' But there was another occasion on which his
prayer was not literally fulfilled ; for it was not the
prayer of faith, nor according to the will of God. Elijah
requested for himself that he might die; and he said, 'It
is enough ; now, O Lord, take away my life; for I am
not better than my fathers.' We know what followed:
the journey to Horeb; the vision in the cave; the lesson
taught him in that dreary lull of his tempestuous life—
that the Lord is not in the wind, the earthquake, nor
the fire, but in the still, small voice; then a new mission,
new hopes, new duties. Such an experience is by
no means unparalleled. Some, probably hundreds in
every generation, have prayed for death ; most often,
perhaps, some young and tender spirit, when overwhelmed with the first real experience of the struggle
and perplexity of life. And God has shown them
that His will was not to grant their prayer: but He
has met them in their agony, and taught and
strengthened them, and led them in ways they
had not known. The soul thus taught must surely
feel that it was wrong and faithless to have prayed
so, and will henceforth be content to wait God's time,
and to put unceasing trust and confidence in His
support. This shows that the religious heart will

not make request to God, against what He has plainly shown to be His will.

Now in this instance, and in the cases hitherto supposed, the increased knowledge of the will of God comes from personal experience, or from the study of the words of Christ. But there is another source of knowledge, which though more outward is not less certain, in the experience of mankind at large, and the ascertained facts of nature. The revelations of history and science must be taken into account, if we would learn what God is teaching us of His own will. And we must seek to know this, if we desire to have true reverence in our prayers.

Furthermore, when we think of prayer as a petition addressed to God, there are some human associations to be avoided. It is only in a figure, for example, that the Apostle speaks of our requests being made known unto Him, who knoweth our necessities before we ask, and our ignorance in asking. Nor can we suppose that the unchangeable and righteous Judge of all the earth will be persuaded, by the most lamentable cry, to do otherwise than as He knoweth to be right, or to change that which His loving wisdom orders, either in His earthly or in His heavenly kingdom ; or that, like some human monarch, the Universal Father will smile only on those who do Him homage.

Thus we are led onwards to the reflection that

O

while *request* is almost though not quite always the outward form of prayer, the inward essence of prayer is aspiration tempered with submission, the act of at once lifting up our hearts and resigning them to God's holy will: and the end of prayer is not merely that we may get the particular thing we ask for, but much rather that we may be ourselves received into the nearer presence of God.

The form of request expresses our consciousness of want and of dependence, not any doubt that He who is able, is also willing to supply our need, if He sees this to be good. But in bringing our desires consciously into His presence, we are really engaged in raising our souls to Him. And in this very act, if done in spirit and in truth, our desires are purified and made more conformable to His will. And so the act of resignation follows closely on that of aspiration.

Thus in learning to pray aright, in turning from the form to the spirit, we pass through the earthly things into the heavenly things, and our prayer thereby becomes more real, because more spiritual. This view of prayer may be illustrated from that which is often spoken of as the correlative of prayer— the divine promise, in the history of which there is a similar growth or transition from the visible to the eternal. Abraham, when he left his home, might seem to be led by temporal promises which were

not adequately fulfilled. Many persons may remember a remarkable though melancholy discourse
on this very subject, entitled the Illusiveness of
Life. But was Abraham deceived, because he lived
in the land of promise as in a strange country?
Not so, unless to receive gold for brass is a decep-
tion : for God himself became to Abraham his
shield, and his exceeding great reward. And so of
all that long mirage of temporal hopes which was
almost but not totally dispelled in the destruction
of Jerusalem. Shall we say that the nation was
deluded to whom they came? Surely not, if the
lesson taught to Elijah was worth learning: not unless
David and Isaiah lived in vain : not if the highest
aspirations of our nature are fulfilled in Him who
shall gather in one all the scattered children of God.
The Hope of Israel is not lost through being transfigured into the Hope of Man.

If prayer were simply a request for the immediate
and visible intervention of the Almighty arm, the
sphere of prayer would become narrowed as that of
human knowledge became enlarged. As Socrates
said, it would be irrational and impious to make
request to God about things which He has placed
in our own power. We cannot ask God to do for
us, what we know that He has given us the power
to do for ourselves; nor can we reverently petition
of Him to suspend a law which we know, as clearly

as we know anything, to be of His appointment. But when prayer is regarded in the more spiritual aspect, there is really nothing which affects our life which may not, or indeed which ought not, to become the subject or the occasion of our prayers. There is not a breath of affection or emotion, not a throb of pain, not one bright hope or shrinking fear, except such as are self-condemned, which we may not unbosom to our Father in the language of prayer; that so the outpourings of our heart may be either corrected and purified, or confirmed by the glad consciousness that they are in accordance with His will. For there is no condition in reality so lonely as that imagined by the poet :

> ‘So lonely ’twas,
> That even God seemed hardly to be there.’

And to the mourner, the desolate, the anxious and careworn soul, the precept of the Apostle to pray unceasingly, opens a boundless treasure-house of comfort, and of life, and strength. And this without assuming, or even expecting, that any outward change of circumstances will come to them as a direct answer to their prayers.

In confirmation of the view that aspiration is the essence, and request only the outward form, of prayer, we may adduce examples of prayer, in which nothing is distinctly asked, and nothing is desired, except the single blessing of union with God. 'O God, Thou art my God, early will I seek Thee: my soul thirsteth for Thee, my flesh also longeth after Thee, in a barren and dry land, where no water is.' 'Lord, Thou hast been our dwelling-place in all generations.' 'As the hart panteth after the water-brooks, so panteth my soul after Thee, O God.' 'Lord, into Thy hands I commend my spirit.' No one of these expressions can be strictly called a request, and yet each of them is of the very essence of prayer.

For prayer is the mysterious act of communion between man and his Maker, which it were vain to attempt to define accurately, but which in proportion as it is real and deep must be in conscious accordance with what is known of God. There are indeed imperfect stages of true feeling, which are not without a blessing—upliftings of the partially enlightened soul in passionate entreaty, or instinctive and unreasoning cries wrung from the more instructed spirit in moments of overwhelming trial or depression, when thought is impossible, and the only refuge from distraction is found in prayer. And none of these can be thought to pass unheeded by Him who quenches not the smoking flax. Moreover, there are many poor in knowledge who are rich in faith. But it becomes those who have entered on the Christian life to press forwards towards perfection, to seek to

have their desires moulded more and more in accordance with their Father's will, and to look upon
the strength and support which they receive in the
act of communion with Him, as an infinitely greater
blessing than any temporal good which He withholds
from them, or any immunity from appointed suffering.
Our comfort in religion would be greatly lessened,
if we did not think of God as being always absolutely
good and wise, and as thinking of us far more than
we can ever think of Him. The very ground of
prayer is cut away if we suppose that God is changed
by prayer. And if he who cometh to God must believe that He exists, he that prayeth to God must seek
to know Him as He truly is, and must desire above
all other things that knowledge of God, which is
life eternal.

There is another consideration which, although not
flowing directly from the text, can never be omitted
when we are speaking of prayer, and which is of more
immediate practical importance than any other—a
consideration which leads by a different path to the
same conclusions with the preceding. And it is
this:—that all true prayer is inseparable from
strenuous energetic action.

When, in following the model which our Lord has
given to us, we look upwards, as children to a father,
day by day for the supply of common wants; when
we say with the Psalmist, 'Thou, Lord, only makest

me to dwell in safety;' when we regard every earthly
blessing, of which our cup is full, as coming to us
immediately from His hand—then we shall also
labour most diligently to provide for those of our
own house, and we shall observe most carefully all
those conditions which regulate health, and secure the
preservation of our lives. And this is no paradox : for
our prayer, our thankfulness, and our practical
obedience are rooted in the same spirit of trust in
God, who teaches us concerning Himself, not only
by the inward motions of the Spirit in man, but by
the outward facts of His providence in the world.
And still more, when we plead for the supply of those
deeper wants, of which the consciousness begins with
the feeling of sinfulness and infirmity, we find prayer
to be inseparable from earnest endeavour. It is
true indeed that even agonized prayer may long
precede the day of final victory and triumph. For
aspiration comes before performance. God is good
to us, even when we have destroyed ourselves. And
even while we are living thoughtlessly, He pre-
pares much within us that is called forth afterwards
into higher life: and when we have begun to seek
Him, it is marvellous how, from a brief and passing
moment of communion, from a broken and confused
and distracted cry, He begins to mould our spirits to
higher aims, and to temper them into gentler forms
than heretofore. Those broken cries were met by

a mightier power. But if we persevere, that power
will also overshadow us when we return to duty. The
new-creating hand of our Father will be still upon
us, and will be felt to encircle us more closely when
again we pray. There is no uncertainty here, for
this is not the question of some outward occurrence
which may or may not be turned to good ; but we are
close to the rock on which we build, and are drawing
ever nearer to the fountain of life. And the certainty
is a growing certainty. To the ripe Christian, whom
God has brought through many trials to the peace
which passeth understanding, this spirit becomes, in
the language of the well-known hymn,

'His vital breath, his native air;'

like the thought of a beloved friend which never
leaves the heart, almost like the abiding consciousness of his individual being. And there are times
and events which fall on younger spirits,

'Whose sudden frost is sudden gain.'

As this spirit grows, the connexion between prayer
and action, of which we have spoken, becomes more
and more closely woven. What was at first a general
aspiration towards the higher life, the desire to be
pure even as Christ is pure, becomes the ruling motive
in all the graver circumstances, and more and more
by degrees in all the circumstances of life. To pray
is to anticipate action : to act is to realize prayer.

And the habit becomes more fixed of lifting up the heart, not at one brief moment, but whenever the Christian is called either to act or suffer, for that support of the everlasting arms, which ministers strength and peace and comfort, which lifts him out of himself and redoubles his energy, giving the present assurance of a future recompense, in the face of which all suffering is light and all labour a blessing.

Further, whatever may be said of prevailing notions respecting intercessory prayer, it is certain that in no act of our religious life, and least of all in prayer, ought our thoughts and wishes to be confined to the narrow circle of our own wants, whether temporal or spiritual. What a glorious inheritance might even a single life become, how rich in great results, how manifold in blessing, were each one repeatedly to think over in the spirit of prayer, to bring consciously before him in communion with the Almighty, all those with whom he has to do—their peculiar wants, their dangers, their opportunities, their weaknesses and how to remedy them, his own shortcomings in dealing with them in time past, his resolutions to make renewed efforts to help them in the future. How would the idea of living for others, which is now often ineffectual because so vague, be in that case intensified and realized! What increase of wisdom should we not receive from Him who

giveth liberally to all, and upbraideth not any! How
would sympathy, intuitive perception, instinctive tact,
and unwearied energy, be multiplied!

Need it be added, finally, that thanksgiving is an
essential part of prayer; or that this element is especially characteristic of our religion, as the religion of
cheerfulness and hope? There is no difficulty here; or
rather the difficulty is of the heart, and not of the head.
If we believe that God is the author of our blessings,
our want of thankfulness to Him in thought and
action, in our lips and lives, can only be regarded
by us as a sin.

There is no fear of our believing too much in the
efficacy of prayer. We believe in it far too little.
We think far too little of the importance of conse-
crating by the spirit of devotion the whole tenour of our
lives. But there is some fear that, by closing our eyes
to what God is teaching us of His own ways through
the history and experience of our race, we may retain
a lower conception of the nature of prayer than is
justified by what God has taught us of Himself; and
that we may take something from the reality of our
prayers by thus separating them from the daily current
of our thoughts, and from the principles that needs
must regulate most things in the ordinary current
of our lives. For if in our so-called secular thoughts
and actions God is regarded by us, as experience has
shown Him to be, as a God of Order, whose Providence

is one with Law, but in our prayers alone we retain the earlier and less perfect notion of a God of caprice and change—then, no less surely than the man whose soul was limed with a bosom sin, 'when we would pray and think, we think and pray to *several* objects.' But if the spirit of true religion contained in the words of Christ is allowed to have free course, it will be found not to contradict, but rather to supplement and enlarge, the lesson of experience and knowledge. In this also Christ came not to destroy, but to fulfil.

SERMON XVI.

THE RIGHTEOUSNESS OF CHRIST.

'Except your righteousness shall exceed the righteousness of the scribes and Pharisees, ye shall in no case enter into the kingdom of heaven.'—MATT. v. 20.

To ears that have been attuned to the sounds of ordinary life, the tone of prophecy even from the lips of Christ comes with somewhat of harshness. Imperfectly apprehending the evils which called forth the utterance, the mind cannot wholly realize the truth and righteousness of that which is uttered. If our modern sensibilities are thus jarred by the woes which our Lord denounced against the teachers of his country and generation, it is right that we should remember (1) not to dwell too much upon the form of words ; these naturally have something in them specially applicable to the time and adapted to the minds of the time : (2) that in the severest of all denunciations there is a tone of pitying expostulation—recalling the lament over Jerusalem, 'If thou hadst known;'—'Ye serpents, ye generation of vipers, how shall ye escape the damnation of hell?' The wish for their escape is even stronger than the almost despair. True moral and spiritual indignation is the outcome of love, and is proportioned to the intensity of love. What depth of sorrowing affection is there not contained in the calm words, 'It were better for him that a millstone were hanged about his neck, and he were drowned in the depths of the sea'? Bearing this in mind, we shall be free to fix our attention on the lasting import of our Lord's prophecy—the irreconcileable opposition between the spirit of Christ and the spirit of hypocrisy and fanaticism ; the spirit which binds heavy burdens grievous to be borne, and touches them not ; which devours widows' houses, while for a show making long prayers ; which takes away the key of knowledge ; which tithes mint, anise, and cummin, while neglecting justice and mercy ; which builds the sepulchres of the righteous, while filling up the measure of the iniquity of those who killed them.

But we should lose something of the historical, and therefore of the real significance of the contrast of Christianity and Pharisaism, were we to dwell exclusively on such passages as these. We know from Scripture that individuals amongst the Pharisees were very far from being mere hypocrites. Nicodemus was a Pharisee, and one of the Sanhedrim ; so was Gamaliel, the human teacher of St. Paul. These, both in different ways, without avowing their belief

in Christ (there is no reason for supposing that Gamaliel was a believer), acted in a manner which is
certainly not recorded for condemnation. We cannot
suppose them to be included in the sweeping net of
the anathemas pronounced upon their class. And
deep students of Eastern literature tell us of facts
which show that these were no mere isolated excep-
tions, facts which to many Christians may come with
surprise.

During the four hundred years and upwards, from
about 200 B.C. to 200 A.D., during which the scribes
were the leaders of the Jewish race, sitting, as our
Saviour truly said, in the seat of Moses, and succeed-
ing to the influence exercised by the schools of the
prophets, there were many wise and good men amongst
them—men who have left sayings worthy to have found
a place in the Book of Wisdom, or the Proverbs of
Solomon, and breathing a pure and exalted morality,
occasionally even something of a prophetic spirit.
For their race and country many of them were content to die. Nor was their zeal for the law a mere
ignorant inculcation of outworn ceremonial precepts.
They at least endeavoured to give a higher meaning
to these precepts while they enforced them. And
some were forward to proclaim, in the spirit of the
prophets, that a blameless life was of more worth
than all outward observances. Speculation and
reflection had not been stationary between the time

of Malachi and that of Christ. Those who have had the curiosity to read the English translation of the Apocrypha are well aware that the 'hope full of immortality' is ascribed to the just with far greater clearness in its pages than in the Old Testament. And he who said, ' Do not unto another what thou wouldest not have another do unto thee. This is the whole law,' was surely not far from the kingdom. To suppose such a man (who, it is said, lived in the generation before our Lord) to be included in the denunciations of the Pharisees, would be a mistake of the same order as to imagine that Socrates and Plato were consciously included by St. Paul in his universal description of the evils of the heathen world in the first chapter of the Epistle to the Romans. ' Not to retaliate ; ' to ' labour without hope of earthly reward ; ' ' to esteem charity before knowledge ; ' ' to be of those who make for peace : ' these and many other such counsels of perfection have something in them almost of a Christian sound.

Almost, and yet not quite. For, first of all, their tone, like that of all morality except the Christian, is negative ; whereas Christianity is wholly positive : and this is really the difference between the finite and infinite. What a difference, for example, between saying with Hillel or Confucius, ' Do not unto another what thou wouldest not have another do unto thee,' and saying, ' Whatsoever ye would that men should

do to you, even so do ye unto them;' between saying,
'Do no harm even to enemies,' as Plato said, and
saying, 'Love your enemies;' between 'It is better to
suffer wrong than to do wrong,' though that was a noble
paradox of Socrates, and 'Bless them that curse you,
do good to them that hate you and persecute you.'

Secondly, and this is the point to which I would
chiefly invite attention, we cannot but mark the
fact that Pharisaism did not, any more than Greek
philosophy, redeem the world: its tendency was
rather on the whole a retrograde tendency. It
had, comparatively speaking, no leavening power.
Individual teachers might strive with much effect to
bring the ancient code into harmony with the wants
of a reflective and cultivated age. Within certain
schools, a lofty esoteric teaching might prevail ; nay,
some even, yearning after the true consolation of
Israel, might by their pure and charitable lives and
their wise precepts put real new wine into the old
bottles : just as the more hopeless attempt was afterwards made by well-meaning heathens to reanimate
the dying form of pagan worship into a fit tabernacle
for a spiritual service. Many a zealous and 'angelic
doctor' may have honestly sought, by instructing his
hearers out of the law, to be a guide to the blind,
a light to those in darkness, an instructor of the
foolish, a teacher of babes, having the form of knowledge and of the truth in the law. But for the pulling

down of the strongholds of evil, another method was
needed, that of Christ.   Such teachers did not sweep
away the mountainous dust of error for truth to over-
peer ; they did but little to melt the pride and fanaticism of the soul.   The breach between man and
man, between Jew and Gentile, between bond and
free, between Pharisee and publican, could not be
healed even slightly with words, however mildly
spoken : to hedge about the Law by however enlightened an interpretation, after the Law had become
a burden to the conscience, was not the way to heal
the breach between man and God.   Think of that
miracle of the world, the growth of early Christianity,
of the Christianity of the New Testament, the Christianity of Christ in Galilee, of St. Paul in the cities
of the Roman world : and you will feel the force of
our Lord's saying that His hearers could not be
His true followers, or receive the gifts which He
brought to earth from His Father in heaven, unless
their righteousness exceeded the righteousness of the
Scribe and Pharisee, even if we esteem that righteousness at the highest rate which history warrants.

As we dwell upon this contrast in the light of facts,
the truth comes home to us with new force that
Christianity is more than a theological doctrine, more
even than a moral and spiritual doctrine.   Christianity
is a life.   The essence of Christianity, the ground of
the mighty power which it has wielded, is not to be

P

sought in isolated sayings of Christ (though these do
contain something of the secret), not in the golden
rule, not in the Lord's Prayer—the wisdom and
piety of mankind had approached, though they had
not attained to the perfection of these—but rather
in the life of Christ, and in the inexhaustible energy
of devoted service which that life communicated to
His Apostles. In the knowledge of that life we have
a treasure which was not possessed by the older
world: and although many a good Jew or heathen
might put Christian men to shame, yet there is a
sense in which every one who struggles, however
imperfectly, to make the ideal of that life his own,
is greater than they. In Christ we believe that life
to be absolutely good. In His followers it is partially
and feebly realized, yet ever growing: a life which is
more than the things on which it feeds, which rises
above current maxims, and is too strong in its freedom to be overawed by authority from the past or
deceived by the cant of the present: a life intensely
individual and personal, yet not resting wholly on any
influence save the truth of God.

Let us dwell for a little while on the nature of this
life, (1) as it is seen in Christ himself, (2) as we may
hope to make it our own.

I. The meaning of the life of Christ can never be
drawn out in words. Its greatness is 'beyond the

reaches of our minds' in two ways: both from the fragmentariness of the record, and the divine fulness of even that which is recorded. Still, though we may perceive them faintly, and represent them still more imperfectly, the lines are clear. The simplicity of the main outlines is no less remarkable than their majesty. For each age, for each individual in proportion to his spiritual grasp, that life has a peculiar lesson ; but it also touches immediately the hearts of all men.

It was, before all things, at once a life for man and a life in God. He was ever with the Father and the Father with Him, yet He ever went forth in love intense and universal for all mankind. These two aspects of the life, the inward and the outward, are inseparable. The depth and universality of His love to men is measured by the completeness of His communion with God. That very communion was for the sake of men : 'For their sakes I sanctify myself, that they also might be sanctified through the truth.' But the very entireness of this dependence on His Father, and of this communication of divine love, rendered Him and the lesson which He taught absolutely free from the influences of the surrounding world. From this cause He taught the people ' with authority, and not as the scribes.' What was true in their teaching He might accept and use as the vehicle of the higher teaching, that flowed from His own spirit. He set up no reaction against tradition or authority, as such; but He accepted nothing on the authority of man. For the outpouring of His love was guided by divine truth and righteousness. Truth and love are in their perfection indeed inseparable: and so also are love and right. For that is not true love that hides or blenches from the truth, nor that which swerves from justice for a partial favour. Three principles then arise immediately from the contemplation of the Gospel record— Love, Truth, and Right.

1. Can we imagine any condition of humanity from which the Love of Christ would have shrunk back; any chamber of human misery too dark for Him to enter with consoling strength; any joy so bright that His presence would not make it brighter; any touch of sorrow too fine for Him to share; any fog of ignorance too dense for His sympathy to penetrate? Is it so very wonderful if, at the very rising of this better Sun, the poor misused demoniac was seen sitting at the feet of Jesus, clothed and in his right mind; if the outcast leper's flesh came back to him, as the flesh of a little child? Or can we wonder if, when many a maimed life had been restored, and many a frozen current had been made to flow, the rumour should have spread abroad that the lame man was leaping as a hart and the tongue of the dumb was singing?

2. Or can we imagine any cause for which Christ would have 'softened the eye of Truth'? Was not this the very temptation which He once and for all overcame in the desert? Was it not this that roused the enmity of His countrymen? 'Ye seek to kill me, a man that have told you the truth which I have heard of God.' 'Because I tell you the truth ye will not believe me.' It was to bear witness to the truth, the truth of the all-embracing fulness of the divine love, that He laid down His life upon the cross. For this was He born, and for this cause came He into the world.

3. The Righteousness of Christ is simply the inter-penetration and harmony of this Truth and Love. This righteousness appeals to no human code, yet is the reverse of arbitrary, and finds an echo in every heart. It is nothing else than mercy and truth encountering in the sphere of action. 'Whosoever is without sin among you, let him first cast a stone.' 'Forbid him not, for there is no man who can do a miracle in my name, that can lightly speak evil of me.' 'Her sins which are many are forgiven her, for she loved much.' 'Take heed that ye offend not one of these little ones. For their angels do always behold the face of my Father who is in heaven.' Such are some of the utterances of the righteousness of Christ.

Now ideas of justice and mercy, and even of truth, have stirred the minds of men in all ages in a fitful and partial way. But never till Christ came were they embodied in a perfect life. In Him they are not ideas, but divine realities, or rather the varying aspects, separable only in thought, of one and the same absolute goodness. This is more than all earthly systems, forms, precepts, traditions, laws. There is a spirit here which has power to pass through the thickest crust of dying and decaying life, and to open a way directly to the light of heaven. Are we not sure that if Christ were to come again on earth, to any country or race of men, to any age of the world, His presence would have the same power of raising up the meek, of abashing the insolent, of relieving the oppressed, of convincing seared hearts of their sin? Would He not equally now as then unravel the web of sophistry with simple truth, and throw off as from an armour of proof eterne the darts of envy and of flattery? Would He have yielded to conventional hypocrisies, to the trammels of caste, to any blinding influence either of poverty or of power? Would His sympathies have been confined to one nation or to one quarter of the globe? And though it were presumptuous to use the name of Christ in connection with modern controversies of opinion, yet we may well believe that, in our more complex as well as in that simpler age, He would still raise the standard of an ideal perfection over against the dominant forms of thought and life,

whether these repose on an imaginary continuity
with the past or on prevailing ideas and maxims.
He would still invite His followers to rest not wholly
on example, authority, or tradition, nor yet wholly
on any fancy or impulse of the hour, but on those
eternal principles of truth and right, of which His life
is the great pattern, as our own hearts teach us to
apply them to the circumstances amongst which we
move.   That may not always be an easy task : the
greater therefore is our need of musing on the Gospel
record till we seem to touch the very heart and
spirit of His life.   Let us be sure that that spirit
would be the same, though every fact and circumstance recorded had been different, however hard
it may be to imagine such a thing.   We may therefore generalize these words of Christ, and think we
hear Him say, ' Except the spirit in which you live,
your principle of conduct, the ideal which animates
you, be higher than the spirit of your age, of your
country, of your class, of your party, of your social
circle, you have individually no hold upon the Christian life.   In so far as you fail of this, in so far you
fail of being my follower.   Yea, many shall come
from the east and from the west—many to whom
Christian schools would fain deny the name of Christian, the outcasts of the churches, perhaps even self-
exiled from the Christian pale—and shall sit down
in the kingdom of heaven ; while the children of the

kingdom shall stand in the twilight or in the outer
gloom.' The name of Christian will not help us any
more than the name of Jew; nor does that Christianity which has its being inwardly consist in the
mere preservation of a deposited tradition. The life
is more than the elements of former life : religion
must be a principle of growth, or it ceases to be
a vital power. The Reformation is a beacon to
remind us that Christian as well as Jewish tradition
may become a noxious burden. Nor is the name
of Reformed or Protestant any charm against this
tendency. The lava crust may again harden, forgetting the latent fires.

There is another and a more comforting aspect of
the same thought. He who said that the cup of
cold water given to the disciple should not lose its
reward, would not reject the feeblest effort made,
whether consciously or unconsciously, in the true
service of God and man. In so far as any, amidst
whatever weakness, have done out of a pure heart
and from simple love, not what was expected of
them, not what they had learnt of others, not what
custom or opinion dictated, but what they saw and
felt to be right and good ; they have partaken in that
same measure of the spirit of Christ. And if they
have done this in simplicity and meekness, in the face
of suffering, dislike, and scorn ; in that same measure
they have known the fellowship of Christ's sufferings.

II. In endeavouring to apply this subject practically we are met by three objections, which I propose to deal with in conclusion.

1. It will be said, Does not such preaching tend to spiritual pride? Is not this a new Pharisaism of separation from men in general? How is this consistent with Christian humility?—There is all the difference in the world between aiming at perfection, and thinking we have attained to or approached it. What more humbling than the contemplation of a perfect model? What so humble as adoring love? The youth who suddenly exclaimed, on seeing a perfect work, ' And I, too, am a painter,' would at that moment have been ready to learn from any one who could teach him any detail of the art. Perfection inspires and kindles, but also subdues.

The Christian glories, but not in himself. He glories in that divine grace and truth which he has seen in Christ, and in which he is invited to share. That call and vision will not let him rest; forgetting what is behind, he can think only of the things before. When he has done all in his little sphere, he knows that he is an unprofitable servant of his Lord. But he too often feels how miserable and poor he is; how full of failure, weakness, and error; nay, that the evil he has done is far greater than the good which he can ever hope to do. At such times he leans humbly upon Christ, feeling that though he has

destroyed himself, yet he has a hope of endless renewal there. But will he therefore exalt himself above
other men, who seem to stand strong and firm apart
from the faith on which he builds ; who, either from
circumstances or from peculiarity of nature, are not
consciously partakers of his hope? No, the feeling
of his own weakness, and the perfection of the object
of his worship, combine to teach him to respect whatsoever he sees anywhere around him that is pure,
honest, lovely, or of good report. He will not pitch
his ambition lower than the aim which his Master
has set. 'If ye salute your brethren only, what do
ye more than others? Be ye perfect, even as your
Father in heaven is perfect.' But as the spur of this
ambition is the cure of *all* stagnancy and limitation,
so it is especially the cure of self-complacency and
pride.

There is another reason why the Christian is
humble: because of the reverence which he learns
from his Master for all which bears the human form.
Love tells us of possibilities in others of which a cold
heart would not dream. St. Paul's charity, for example, saw his converts not only as they were, but
as they might become. And was it not his love also,
and his reverence for human nature, which led him
to become all things to all men, that he might by
all means win some? It is pride which keeps up
the barriers between man and man. When charity

has thrown these down, and overflowed them, there is no more room for pride.

2. Another objection comes from a different quarter. Some will tell us that the ideal which we are setting up is after all partial and one-sided ; that Christianity only fosters the passive virtues, such as humility, purity, forgiveness of injuries, patience under provocation, and the like ; and has thus only fostered a weak and puling type of humanity. It needs to be supplemented, they will say, from the annals of human heroism. Whence do we derive our notions of courage, patriotism, and other active virtues ? Is it not rather from ancient and secular history, than from our religion ? And yet an ideal which fails to include these cannot be so perfect as you say. Others will point us to the monuments of Christian bigotry, and will ask, Is this the religion which you say rejoices in the truth ? Did not the idea of truth at first come to men from ancient Greece ? Has it not been quickened into an irrepressible life by the revelations of modern science ?

Now this whole class of objections appears to me to rise from a very natural confusion between the Christianity of the New Testament and the Christianity of the sects ; that is, between the gradual development of our religion in the history of the world, and the religion as it lay at first in unsoiled purity in the mind and heart of its Founder. Great as Christianity has been, the religion of Christ is greater. And surely it is not a chimerical hope that Christianity may become more and more imbued with the spirit of Christ. However this may prove, there is no form of goodness which that spirit will not be found to sanction and to inspire. And true Christianity will be wherever that spirit works and dwells. To say this is not to deny that the world could ill spare any of her greatest and best sons, or afford to forget the lesson which any sage or hero has left behind him. Nor is it to deny that for several virtues we have to thank several climes and peoples. To speak of the life of Christ as virtuous, would be a misuse of language ; because it would be applying praise to that which is above praise. But there is no human virtue which the love, the truth, the righteousness of Christ will not inspire and draw out into a nobler form. Christianity is a religion for the weak, not because Christ is weak, but because He is so strong, because ' to them that are weak He increaseth strength.' Do we seek for courage, for dignity, for fiery indignation, for wisdom not to be entangled by guile, for a firm bearing in denouncing wrong, for strength to act alone, for love of country, for fortitude in bearing pain, for tenderness, for hopefulness, for constancy in friendship, for unshrinking devotion to a noble cause, for universality of sympathies ; and shall we be told by men who have read

the Gospels that these things are not in Christ? Or
do we seek support in maintaining some truth which
has not yet found acceptance in the world, or confirmation in the faith that all true knowledge is
from God; and is it not something to remember
Him who said, in the face of Jewish prejudice, ' My
Father worketh hitherto and I work,' who witnessed
before Pontius Pilate a good confession for the truth?

3. Lastly, some will say, The ideal of the Christian
life is noble and beautiful, but impossible to realize.
Each is so bound in by circumstances in his little
sphere, that it is mockery to tell him to rise beyond
it; and it is more comforting to rest in the assurance
of the well-known hymn,—

> ' The daily round, the common task,
>   Will furnish all we need to ask.'

True, every life must be relative to its circumstances.
The life of Christ himself was not out of harmony
with the conditions of His earthly being. But the
spirit of a life need not be determined by its surrounding atmosphere. And there is no position of life, even
in a Christian country, where the tendency to do
as others do, to fall mechanically into the ways and
maxims of our class or neighbourhood, is not a temptation to be resisted; in which the consistent determination to be guided always by the love of God
and man would not effect a marvellous revolution.
Nor are there any circumstances, however mean,

where there are not opportunities for doing something
to raise men out of a mere unconscious routine, and
to draw out what is best in them by active sympathy.
Those best acquainted with the annals of the poor
could tell us of lives, under more unfavourable circumstances than any of ours, more fruitful, and more
rich in blessing, than many a ministry. He that
is faithful in few things is faithful also in much. The
tradesman who rises above the common practices
of trade in a small town, would be incorruptible if
trusted with the commissariat of a great army. Those
who help to preserve harmony in some obscure circle
of society, might equally help to purify a court. The
labourer who, under the pressure and distress of
poverty, and in the midst of vice and squalor, has
brought up his family in honesty, industry, and purity,
has done as much as if with proportionate advantages
he had raised the morality of a whole kingdom.

Let each, wherein he is called, therein abide *with
Christ:* not seeking to change the outward circumstances of his life, nor straining after originality or eccen-
tricity; yet ever pressing forwards and seeking to rise
above his own past self, and above the level of custom,
education, and habit, and also to raise others ; following the example of our Master Christ, who came to
seek and to save the lost, and freely laid down His
life that He might take it again ; who was lifted from
the earth that He might draw all men unto Him.

SERMON XVII.

REDEEMING THE TIME.

1871.

'See then that ye walk circumspectly, not as fools, but as wise. *Redeeming the time, because the days are evil.* Wherefore be ye not unwise, but understanding what the will of the Lord is.'— EPHES. V. 15—17.

TIMES of agitation and anxiety, whether in our public or private life, seem to throw a new light on the page of Scripture. For what is Scripture but the record of times many and various when the human heart was deeply moved, and with its longings, its regrets, and fears, was with more than usual earnestness feeling after God? Hence it comes that, when the depths of human nature are broken up afresh, and the floods of ungodliness make us afraid, and we desire to speak but know not what to say, we turn with renewed interest to the Old and New Testaments; to find there deep calling unto deep; a more intense experience, giving new powers of thought and feeling to our own; a faith in the One Eternal Being, at once animating and reproving our weaker faith; to find in the New Testament especially a

light of guidance for the troubled spirit, which may
be a lamp to our feet in the perplexity of the darkest
day. The words of holy men of old glow with fresh
meaning for us, as if they had been written yesterday.
For have not we too in modern Europe had our
searchings of heart? Have not we too heard the cry
of innocent blood? Have not we too seen to be
made of a city an heap, and the palace of strangers to
be no city? And even in a period of comparative
tranquillity and outward peace, we ought to think
more seriously than we do of the lessons of experience that have been taught mankind within our own
memory. For what are wars and rumours of wars,
what are the outbreaks of political and social crime,
what are the revelations of wide-spread human misery,
but voices out of the eternal, appealing to the higher
and nobler self in every one of us, and demanding
from us whatever service our nature, training,
and opportunities have made us most capable of
rendering?

I do not much care as a rule for refining upon
the mere words of the Bible. But there is perhaps
something to be learnt by it in the present instance.

The words of the text in the English Version have
become proverbial, 'Redeeming the time;' but the
words of the original, although they would hardly
bear to be differently translated, are even more ex-
pressive. 'Buying up the opportunity,' i.e. 'Not

missing anything of what the passing moment has to give.' And if the call is significant, so also is the reason of the call, 'because the days are evil.' To some men the feeling that they have fallen on evil days has an enervating and paralysing effect. They spend their time in enquiring why the former days were better than these, or torment themselves and others with timorous apprehensions concerning the future. Not so reasoned, not so acted, the leaders of the early Christian congregation. Although 'the days closed around them and the years,' although they thought that the world in which they lived was doomed to destruction coming suddenly in an instant, yet this made to them only more imperative the duty of proclaiming the good news of the kingdom of heaven, of using this world as not abusing it, of living to the glory of God. And although they looked for the sudden appearing of the Son of man coming in the clouds of heaven, and hoped while yet alive to be caught up with Him into glory, they were not selfishly absorbed in that expectancy (those who were so are sternly rebuked by St. Paul), but only sought the more earnestly to bring all men to the knowledge of the truth. Their life was dominated by the spirit and example of Christ, who had looked forth calmly over the long vista of the coming ages, sorrowing indeed for the present, but providing by His own life and teaching an inexhaustible inspiration for the future,

and confidently anticipating the final triumph of His
Father's truth and love.

And if the same spirit is amongst us still, making
those who partake of it in any measure to be as He
was in the world, it will be like a sharp goad within
them, ever driving them onward to 'redeem the time.'
The love of country, the love of kindred, the nobler
ambition, the delight of spontaneous energy, will all
be quickened and revivified by this higher motive
power, that will give new meaning to all.   And this
motive will itself be greatly intensified by the consideration that the opportunities which are now before
us may ere long have passed away for ever.   The
opportunity certainly will not be the same ten years
hence as it is to-day : but more than this, if we neglect
the present, the evils we contend with may have become too strong for any remedy.   In this sense the
words of the New Testament, that 'now is the accepted time,' that 'the time is short,' or 'urgent,'
have a special applicability to the days in which
we live.

There are not wanting signs which cast a shade of
uneasiness on the wisest hearts ; there are unmistakeable changes—silent revolutions they are sometimes
called—which rouse mingled feelings of regret and
hope ; and there are ideal aspirations having promise
of endless blessing, but which like new wine are apt to

kindle madness in precipitate minds. In the midst of this uncertain light the Christian will try to 'walk circumspectly, not as foolish but as wise;' endeavouring to understand the will of his Lord; endeavouring to learn how he may best help to realize the presence of Christ on earth; so living apart from society that he may serve men better; so becoming all things to all men that he may promote what is best for all; so labouring that his work may not all be lost in the days that are to be.

When we hear or read of the sad increase of poverty that has grown side by side with the accumulation of wealth, of the dangerous effects of ignorance and discontent, of the brutality of some classes and the vacant self-indulgence of others amongst our fellow-countrymen, our first thought is apt to be, What can we do? We have not the knowledge to find out a cure for social maladies; we have not power to give effect even to what we know. We have no firm hold either on the present or the future. The political and moral forces of our age are too many for us and too strong. Feeling our ignorance and blindness, we are sometimes tempted to relax all effort and to drift with the tide. And it is true that as individuals severally we can do very little. But that is the reason why we should all together resolve to be up and doing, to awake and live. The truly wise and courageous spirit knows

how to turn the cries of panic and alarm into a source
of encouragement and strength.

> ''Tis true that we are in great danger :
> The greater therefore should our courage be.'

The man who so reasoned knew how to find 'the
soul of goodness in things evil.' And it is time that
those who have the blessings of education and enlightenment within their reach should consider, not
the danger to themselves and their own class,
although this may be also an element in the question, but the dangers to the future of mankind which
are inherent in the present and past condition of
society: not with selfish and unreasoning panic fears,
as men of old, when they saw the waters of the
flood rising, built dams and dykes to keep it out;
but with an active faith in the power of truth and
righteousness, as of the sun in his strength, even yet
to renew the face of the earth.

Here are, it may be, five hundred persons; not a
great number; insignificant when compared with the
population of one of our great towns, a mere drop in
the ocean when compared with the population of the
smallest country in Europe. And yet if not one such
company but several in each of our great centres of
industry were strongly united in the determination
to redeem this time, to buy up the present opportunity, to recover something from the shallowness and
frivolity, the selfishness and meanness, the hurtful

extravagance, the indifference and coldness of our day—a great change might be produced in a few years. And it would be hard to exaggerate the importance of the occasion, or to estimate the consequences that may flow from the spirit shown by educated persons in a critical time. Christianity was in its first origin the religion of the poor and the oppressed. Could it become not in name only but in deed the religion of the rich, of those whose opportunities are so great, whose material resources are so vast, as those of the wealthier classes in the present day, what might not be effected by Christianity, not as a mere religious sentiment but as a principle of action; a principle not opposed to reason, but inviting help from all the culture and enlightenment of the world!

Is it inconceivable that the dreary sense of vacancy which begins to oppress those who have most leisure, may some day amount to a degree of spiritual poverty that may again lead multitudes to the kingdom of heaven? Are there not signs that it is so already? Are there not many who are sighing to do service to humanity, if they could only find a way? There is a sense in which it is still true that it is hard for the rich to enter into the kingdom. But not until they have so entered in can the kingdoms of the world become the kingdoms of Christ and God.

Whether the renewal is to come from the richer
or the poorer classes, or from various parts at once,
it is sure to arise in some way from a sense of need.
And a true feeling of the evils of our age, which are
really those of every age, not conceived in any
alarmist spirit, but on a calm estimate of all that
is dark in the present and dim and uncertain in the
future, may be to all of us a constant spur rousing
us ever anew to redeem the time. For the first
step on this upward path is that each one of us for
himself should be resolved to make the most of life.
If every one of five hundred persons were fully and
practically convinced of this, the effect would be far
greater than the proportion of that number to the
whole. One will that is guided by a noble and consistent purpose is a match for many that are dissi-
pated by idleness or sunk in sloth. And the call
is or should be loudest to those whose opportunities
are the greatest, who are richest in the most valuable
of possessions, the possession of time: I mean those
who are still young. You know not to what duties, to
what sacrifices, to what great efforts you may be called
hereafter; but you have each one of you a career before
you. It may be long or short, bright, dark, or chequered,
who can tell? In that career you have of course a
personal interest. But it is well for you to remember,
for it is an inspiring thought, that that personal
interest is not all. On your learning all you can,

on your growth in every sort of activity and energy,
on the development amongst you of a healthy public
spirit and an elevated moral tone, on your keeping
yourselves pure from evil, a great deal more depends
than what is commonly called your success in life.
It is right that you should have this aim before you,
for it is on personal motives that higher motives are
built up, and it is nobler to think even of one's own
future than to be lost in momentary pleasures ; but
you must also remember that even in your earthly
vocation a higher calling than this is yours. The
world has need of you, your brethren of mankind have
need of you, and God would have you minister to
their need : not that you should gain and spend and
live as burdens to the ground ; not that you should
dream away the time in sentiment, whether earthly
or spiritual ; not that you should gratify a poor ambition to make a name, and stir about you where you
live a little dust of praise : but that you and such as
you are should be a strength and not a weakness to
this people in the hour that is coming on ; that whatever may be the work in which you are called to
serve God and man, it may be done faithfully and
wisely, without personal respects, without narrow
prejudices, with unsparing effort, with large sympathy ;
that it may be guided by the noblest aims, as being
done by those who are not unwise, but understanding
what the will of the Lord is, who know the good and

welcome it from afar off, who know the evil in its beginnings and not only when it blossoms out in sin.

For, in the next place, as the Apostle warns us, in order to redeem the time, to buy up the opportunity, we must seek to understand the problem of our age: in other words, we must ask what our Lord would have us now to do as Christians.

The problem of the first age of Christendom was to gather out of all nations a peculiar people, to shield the young congregation from the corruptions of heathenism, as well as to emancipate them from Jewish superstition. Hence the frequent call to the first Christians to come out and be separate from the world. The duty of our own age is in some respects the opposite of this, not to separate but to draw men together: to diffuse the treasure that was saved to us in the ark of the early Church: to bring all the rays of goodness and truth that shine upon us from the past, or from distant lands, into one focus; to harmonize them through a liberal application of the spirit of Christ ; and to make them to be seen and known of all men: that so those mighty powers and instincts of humanity, that would else act blindly and destructively, may be drawn forth by the magnetic charm of goodness and truth to act gently and beneficently for mankind; just as the same force which cleaves the oak asunder, and shatters towers, and deals instantaneous death, has been applied to

bind east and west together, and to be the messenger
of human utilities over the globe. The study of
inanimate nature has done this for us; and it is only
when, by the candid study of the social and political
forces of humanity in our own time, we have learnt to
render them the instruments of love and righteousness, and not of hatred and immeasurable revenge,
that we can be truly said to be not unwise, but understanding what the will of the Lord is. It was after
all a sort of accident that the first Christians had to
separate themselves from the heathen world, from the
other Jewish sects, from the early heretics. The essential aim of Christianity was always much rather to
combine, to pull down walls of partition, to make
both one—both the mystical monotheistic spirit that
soared above the world to seek for God in an unseen
heaven, and the spirit that went forth responsively
towards the broken lights of His mirrored glory, as
the invisible things of Him were made clearly seen in
Nature. And we cannot err in thinking that God is
calling us in this present age to diffuse as widely as
possible every element of good; to draw class and
class together, or rather to draw together man and
man: not by the sudden and violent abolition of pri-
vilege; not by despising what is good in itself, because
it happens to have been associated with the preroga-
tives of a few; but by turning the pride of the few
into the blessing of the many; by laying unreservedly

open all that can instruct or elevate mankind ; by giving all a common interest in every inheritance of the past; by partaking without unworthy shrinking in every honest aspiration for the future.

We know that the future is, as the past has been, in the hands of God, who is working all together for a purpose that is full of blessing. He has given us much knowledge and many resources that were denied to former times. And yet we cannot feel that we are better than our fathers, or that we have any right to expect to be exempt from those violent drawbacks, those sudden shocks, in which, as history teaches us, the accumulated penalties of former errors are often brought on one generation. Let us then make full use of the opportunity, and eagerly buy up the golden hours while they last, ἐξαγοραζόμενοι τὸν καιρόν, in the deeply grounded hope and faith that even this age may be made a means of blessing to the coming ages ; but should we be disappointed of that hope, that we may at least be faithful soldiers of the Lord of men, and may be conscious of His eternal blessing.

For, lastly, the Christian aim and motive is not bounded by the horizon of time : and although it is false to say of us that we are neglecting this world for another, it is true that in our use of this world we are striving to gather a more lasting treasure. And we believe that every true endeavour on the side of good, every right word and noble act, though it may fail of earthly continuance, though it may find no acceptance amongst men, has yet a place amongst the eternal things, and is of enduring value in the sight of God.

SERMON XVIII.

DESTROYING AND FULFILLING.

'Think not that I am come to send peace on earth: I came not to send peace, but a sword.'—MATT. x. 34.

'Think not that I am come to destroy the law, or the prophets; I am not come to destroy, but to fulfil.'—MATT. v. 17.

'To this end was I born, and for this cause came I into the world, that I should bear witness unto the truth.'—JOHN xviii. 37.

THERE are several modes of handling the Scriptures which for centuries had great fascination for ingenious minds, but may now be said almost to have passed away. One of these was the attempt to produce what was called a harmony of the Gospels: that is, so to arrange and bring together the statements of the different Evangelists, identifying what can be shown to be identical, explaining apparent discrepancies, distinguishing what though similar is not the same, as while maintaining

the infallibility of each narrator, to present the contents of all four in one full, continuous, and harmonious
narrative.   Little has been heard of such attempts of
late.   I am not aware that any considerable author
now living sets before himself the problem exactly
in this way.   Many good religious people now-a-days
have never seen a ' Diatessaron,' as such a work is
technically called.

The fact is that these very studies, and others
kindred to them, have disproved the assumption on
which such attempts were based.   They have helped
to show us the true nature of the book we are
studying, which renders such a forced harmony impossible.   The Gospels are fragmentary records, con-
taining divers branches of one or perhaps of two
streams of early tradition.   The order they follow
is often not the order of time, and different Evangelists have arranged even the same materials on a
different plan.

But while such an external unity is unattainable,
and if attained would be barren of any spiritual result,
there is a deeper harmony, not of the Gospels only
but of the whole New Testament, and in a certain
sense also of the whole Bible, which in these days
well deserves our earnest search—the harmony, not of
detail, but of spirit.

In seeking for this also we shall encounter difficulties
and objections, which must not be merely set aside,

and which may remind us that the harmony for which we look is not simple unison, but the concord of many different tones. The idea of a growth or progress in the revelation of the Old Testament, and of a further progress from the Old Testament to the New, an idea already implied in Christ's own teaching, has been the solution of much perplexity, and has made the Bible more instructive to us because more living. But this does not help us when we are considering the words of Christ himself, as they are reported in the New Testament. We have then to bear in mind that what we see is only the reflex image, and that the same light, however clearly reflected, will be seen differently in surfaces that have a slightly different form. Still, whatever · variety, or even divergence, a minute historical criticism may bring out in the records of our Lord's ministry, this does not affect our reasonable conviction that His spirit dominates the whole; and hence, in comparing different words of Christ, and endeavouring to draw from them one comprehensive and consistent lesson, we are not entering on an irrational inquiry, if only there be nothing irrational in our method of pursuing it.

One important condition of such a method is that nothing shall be explained away. For instance, if it is said that Christ came indeed to send only peace on earth, but that, because of the wickedness of men, when He laboured for peace they made them ready to battle: that would be to soften away unwarrantably the meaning of the first of the verses which we have read. On the other hand, when an extreme thinker of the second century, the so-called heretic Marcion, contended that Christ had really said, 'Think not that I am come to fulfil the law or the prophets; I am not ·come to fulfil, but to destroy,' he was guilty of a still more reprehensible perversion of the text of the second verse. Each saying must be allowed to stand forth in full individuality in all the original freshness of colour and distinctness of outline: and then, if there appear any difference or opposition, this will be provocative of genuine thought, and may lead us to the contemplation of some higher and wider principle, in which the opposition is at once justified and done away.

The two verses which we have taken from the first Gospel certainly present the advent or coming of Jesus Christ in two very different aspects. In the one, His work is spoken of as disorganizing, separating, destroying; in the other, as reconstructing, reconciling, fulfilling. In the one it is described as negative, in the other as positive, in its effects. Yet both sayings are recorded substantially by the same witness, and both have, if we may venture to say so, strong internal evidence of genuineness.

What then is the ground of the contrast?

This may perhaps appear if we place both sayings side by side, in the light of those deep and comprehensive words which are characteristically recorded in the fourth Gospel, 'To this end was I born, and for this cause came I into the world, that I might bear witness unto the truth.' Taking this declaration for our guide, we may be able to see that the ministry of Christ, in bearing witness to the truth, could not immediately bring peace on earth, but must for a time bring division; and yet that, in the end and consummation, that same ministry could not be opposed to any existing element of good, but must draw all forth, and complete them, and make them pure and fruitful.

I. Consider the relation in which Christ and His followers were placed towards His contemporaries by His coming to bear witness to the truth.

He did not court attention. He did not strive nor cry, nor make His voice to be heard in the streets. He simply taught, as He had opportunity, those who felt their need of teaching, and healed those who had need of healing, answered openly questions that were asked in public, conversed in private with His chosen friends, and when urged with unreal scruples exposed their fallacy by a few wise trenchant words; and yet in three years the cross was ready for Him, and a few years later the hour of persecution was ripe for the infant Church. Does this seem strange? Then we have yet to learn, that while our Lord's teaching was the gentlest, it was also the most searching, the most uncompromising that has ever been heard on earth. He knew no terms with evil or falsehood in any form. The moment His words touched them, they were stripped of their disguises and shown in manifest deformity. The parable of the leaven is indeed an apt description of the imperceptibly gradual progress of the truth, in the course of ages and over the world; but the direct utterances of Christ are rather to be compared to the two-edged sword, piercing even to the dividing asunder of the soul and spirit. When He quietly but openly persisted in healing on the sabbath-day, when He sat down with the publican, when He turned from the scribes to the multitude and said 'Hear and understand,' He was rousing against Himself the prejudices of His countrymen in all their might, no less effectually than in His final denunciation of the 'blind Pharisee.' It is evident on the mere surface of the history that He deliberately and repeatedly, both in His words and actions, cut right athwart many of the most cherished religious feelings of His countrymen.

Now, were it not for the mere habit of reverential acquiescence in all that our Saviour said and did, some would here be ready to ask whether a milder course would not have been possible. There were excellent men amongst the Jewish doctors, men whose

R

utterances deserved to be written in letters of gold, who taught a pure morality, and adapted their interpretation of the law and the prophets to the wants of a reflective age. Might He not have quickened and vitalized by His divine influence the teaching of these purer schools; and thus have adopted what was good in the minds of His countrymen, while only indirectly suppressing and ignoring the evil? Could He not thus have gently insinuated the high truths which He came to teach mankind, and caused them ultimately to prevail, without any need for the offence to come, without the battle to the utterance, without casting fire upon the earth, or accomplishing His baptism of blood? Not in this way did He reason who came to save the world. He chose not to entrust the new wine to the old bottles. He saw those whom the refined doctrines of the schools could never reach, ' how they fainted and were scattered abroad, as sheep having no shepherd,' and He opened His mouth and taught them; He saw how custom lay on men like frost, and He inspired them with truths that made them free; He saw the kingdom of heaven open, and bade men enter in; He healed the life that had been maimed and distorted by the oppressions of the time; He said to the chief of sinners, 'Repent and be forgiven;' He knew the infinite love of His Father, and He extended that love in speech and action to the outcast and despised. Hence came the conflict unto death, in which the powers of fanaticism. and worldly craft, and selfishness in high places seemed to crush out the life of the Son of man, and were themselves for ever crushed. Hence also His followers, who had left home and friends and lands for His Gospel's sake, were persecuted from city to city; and five were in one house divided, three against two, and two against three.

II. In that hour the old things passed away, and all things were becoming new. And yet it is no less certain that He came not to destroy, but to fulfil The force of these words has been greatly impaired by a mechanical system of types and antitypes, with which the fancy of interpreters has interlaced the Old and New Testaments. But the real connection between them is of a deeper kind, which is expounded in the Sermon on the Mount. The separate commandments in the old law might all be deduced from the one law of love: only they forbade, while love inspires; they prescribed actions, love is an inward principle; they were limited and subject to exception, love is infinite, universal, and eternal. Hence, when Christ proclaimed the absoluteness of the law or spirit of love, He was not destroying the essence of the Mosaic law. Much rather He gave free course to the eternal thought of which that law had been the local and temporary expression, so that the living water that was for the healing of the nations, but had

been artificially confined for the supposed benefit
of the chosen people, might well forth afresh and in-
exhaustibly, and be found enough for the supply of
the whole world. The commandment, 'Thou shalt
love thy neighbour,' was no new commandment, but
an old commandment, which they had heard from the
beginning. But this, 'Love your enemies, that ye
may be the children of your Father which is in
heaven, for He is kind to the unthankful and the
evil': 'Be ye perfect, even as your Father is perfect,'—
this was a new commandment, with a new and unheard-of sanction, and yet one in which the old commandment was only extended and 'fulfilled.' And
as Moses had proclaimed to Israel, 'The Lord, merciful and gracious, forgiving iniquity, transgression,
and sin, yet by no means clearing the guilty:' so
Christ more authoritatively and more perfectly revealed to all mankind their Father in heaven, who
seeth in secret, whose kingdom is open to all that
come repenting of their sins, and hungering and thirst-
ing after righteousness. And as the prophets, when
the Mosaic law was already becoming a burden of unmeaning ceremonies, had sought to rouse men with
many voices to a belief in the righteousness and
faithfulness of the Most High; and declaring that
mercy was better than sacrifice, had cried aloud,
'Cease to do evil, learn to do well, seek judgment,
relieve the oppressed, judge the fatherless, plead for

the widow,'—so Jesus, when the same deadening crust had still further hardened on the conscience of the Jew, proclaimed with greater fulness and authority the same everlasting lesson. 'Not he that saith unto me, Lord, Lord, shall enter into the kingdom of heaven, but he that doeth the will of my Father who is in heaven.' 'Not that which goeth into the mouth defileth a man, but that which cometh out of the mouth, from the heart, defileth a man.' 'The kingdom of heaven is within you.' 'Many shall come from the east and from the west, and shall sit down with Abraham and Isaac and Jacob in the kingdom of heaven.' In such sayings there lies the promise of a kingdom of righteousness far greater, because more universal, than had been dreamt of by any Hebrew prophet. And yet in them the inmost spirit of the prophetic utterances is enlarged and fulfilled.

And now the teaching of Christ is to us an inheritance from the past, as that of Moses and Isaiah was to the contemporaries of Christ himself. And we have no one teacher who can be to us in the place of Christ, no infallible interpreter of His mind and will. Nor is our inheritance a simple one, nor is it an easy task for us to appropriate His teaching as a rule of life. The theologies of three great epochs come between us and the precious relics of His instruction which survived the first century of our era. The

experience and modes of thought of a Western Euro-
pean people, industrial, progressive, practical ; the
history of so many ages, including the diverse phases
of historical Christianity; above all, the growth of
science, and the revolution it has caused in man's ideas
of the world he lives in and of his own origin and
destiny—all seem to unfit us for learning from Christ
with the simplicity of the early Church.   And therefore, if there is a spirit now at work, not, as once
in Christ, with divine fulness in some one mind, but
with various excellences in many different minds,
yet essentially one with His, destined spiritually
to renew the face of the world, to make a new beginning of the religious life, and to bring a time of
refreshing from the presence of God — that spirit
must at first, like His, send abroad on earth not
peace, but a sword: and for the same reason,
because it will be prompted wholly by the love of
truth.

For it is not always possible to enjoy the combined
blessings with which the Hebrew monarch comforted
himself in his decline, when he said, ' There shall be
peace and truth in my day.'   It was not possible
for the generation to which Christ came.   The voice
that cried, ' Peace on earth,' was prophetic of the last
result : there was another prophecy that described the
nearer future, ' He is set for the fall and rising again
of many in Israel, and for a sign that shall be spoken

against; yea, a sword shall pierce through thine own soul.'

It was not possible for the Reformation period. How earnestly the warm heart of Luther often longed for quiet, peaceful days; but he and the other reformers were urged onwards by the claims of truth and by a spirit which they durst not resist, to provoke the opposition of powerful enemies, and to live in endless strife and contention.

And in the present age, the candid love of truth has often brought, and will yet bring, not peace, but rather division. There are no martyrs now-a-days, and persecution has dwindled to a mockery of its former self: but yet any one who sets himself simply to know the truth and to proclaim what he knows, is likely to give deep offence to many persons, and if he is of a sensitive nature, to receive many a sharp wound. There is nothing amongst us to compare to the tribulation of the first Christians, or the fiery trial through which the reformers passed : but honest thought on religious subjects has in many ways given rise to separation, misunderstanding, distrust, and bitterness. This partly arises from the importance which men justly attach to religion. Who will deny that the earnest inquiry on matters connected with theology, which has such an absorbing interest for many of us, has introduced into society an element of discord ; that difficulties in family life, the cooling or decay of friendships, even something of moral injury to weak characters, may be indirectly traceable to this cause ; or that there are peculiar drawbacks which attend the teaching of religion in a time of transition ?

Hence comes the frequent outcry against negative teaching ; a complaint indeed most natural on the part of those whose positions are likely to be denied. But quite apart from controversy, many gentle, true-hearted people are found to say: Do not destroy until you are able to build ; unless you can give something, do not take away.

But to speak thus is to forget the necessarily partial character of all human endeavours in the elaboration of truth. In Christ alone there is perfect fulness and proportion. We cannot hope that it will be given to the same persons amongst us to clear the ground and to crown the edifice. But when some have laboured, there will be others who will enter into their labours.

I will here say a word in defence of negative theology : all will have many opportunities of hearing what can be said against it. Unless we suppose that there are no clouds of superstition, no mists of error to obscure the beams of the sun of righteousness and truth, we cannot hope that his rising on us will be perfectly serene. There will be a struggle of the light with the darkness before the light shines clearly on our path.

Therefore it is not enough to say in condemnation of a teacher that his work is negative. It may be partial and incomplete for that reason; but if he is earnest and sincere, he may still be doing in his measure a good and necessary work. We have lately sung in reference to the Advent of the Son of man:

> 'He comes, the prisoners to release,
>   In Satan's bondage held;
> The gates of brass before Him burst,
>   The iron fetters yield.'

That is the description of a negative process. The denial of purgatory, of the sacrifice of the mass, of indulgences, of the possibility of 'buying corrupted pardon of a man,' was a great part of the work of the Reformation.

The form of negation or disproof has at least this merit, that it arrests attention, it is unequivocal, it is unmistakeable as far as it goes. The mere suggestion of new ideas may reach the ear and conscience of a few; but the denial of old falsehoods is more intelligible to the many.

But then all negation that is fruitful in result is in effect the affirmation of a higher principle, and that not because of novelty, but because of truth. The breaking of the clod, the bursting of the sheath, the shedding of the husk, these are but the outward signs of growth and of the stirring of the mysterious life within. And it may be that a higher intelligence,

looking down upon the distractions of our age, might
see in them the signs of a larger growth, the beginnings of a nobler life for man. It may be that this
larger and nobler life shall be the fulfilment of Christianity, as Christianity is the fulfilment of the law ;
and that the religious teacher of the coming age, like
the instructed scribe in our Lord's parable, will bring
out of his treasure-house thoughts that are at once
new and old.

It may be that the alteration of some old beliefs
is one of many ways by which we are being
brought back to a simple faith in God ; by which
is meant not only the conviction that He is, and
that He is the rewarder of those that seek Him,
but the trust in His perfect righteousness and
equity, in His faithfulness to all His creatures, in
His goodness being over all His works, in His willingness to impart of His own righteousness to all
conscious beings. This faith is no mere speculative idea, but, where it exists in any strength, is the
most powerful of all principles of action, making the
love of God convertible with the love of man, and
turning the love of man into a life of self-devotion
for man's highest good. Now what is this but the
central principle of the New Testament, the Gospel
which Christ taught, the faith of Christ which St. Paul
found all-sufficing? It had to contend with Jewish
narrowness then ; it may still have to contend with

theological and ecclesiastical narrowness of more recent origin. But as other doctrines and traditions are
thrown into the background, this first principle of all
theology, viz. that God is good, that He is light and
that in Him is no darkness at all ; this essence of our
Lord's teaching, ' Be ye perfect, even as your Father
is perfect,' and also this, ' Inasmuch as ye have done it
unto one of the least of these my brethren, ye have
done it unto me.'—will only be seen in clearer light,
and the assurance of this faith will gain indefinitely
in purity and strength. Then will be the great
triumph of Christianity; and it may prove that, as
has been said by one who has incurred no small
blame as a negative theologian, we may yet be only
at the commencement of the career of Christ as the
great Spiritual Conqueror, even in this world.

For, lastly, this faith will act in harmony with
another great power, which also is from God, which
has sometimes seemed, but only seemed, opposed
to faith, the power of knowledge. Then those great
words, ' I came to bear witness to the truth,' will
receive new force and meaning, the truths of experience being added to those of faith. When a pure
and simple faith has acknowledged freely that all
true science is from God, then science, which also has
(as Bacon said) the spirit of a little child, will again
receive the lesson of faith ; and the two combined,
faith giving the motive and science the means, faith

with love and hope inspiring and impelling, science enlightening, guiding, and ministering, will make a wider and more blessed conquest of humanity than has yet been seen. Then truth shall flourish on the earth, as righteousness hath looked down from heaven. Then 'mind and soul, according well, will make one music as before, but vaster.' Then every principle of good and right which the world has ever known, will have fulfilment, not in asserting their separate and limited titles to acceptance, but through being united with that, than which nothing higher can ever be revealed, the law of Christian love. Then every aspiration of 'the prophetic soul of the wide world dreaming on things to come' shall find satisfaction in the fuller revelation of God.

SERMON XIX.

THE MORAL ELEMENT IN GREEK CULTURE CON-
SIDERED IN RELATION TO CHRISTIANITY.

AN ADDRESS TO STUDENTS.

Introduction.

THE ethics of the New Testament are necessarily indefinite, not only because of the fragmentariness of the record, but because the life recorded consisted so largely in aspiration. Hence the often quoted saying, that 'The Gospel lays down principles rather than rules.' The great outlines stand forth unmistakeably and indelibly: love to God and man; giving more blessed than receiving; the inexhaustible value of faith, hope, and charity. But the application of these principles in the Epistles is necessarily partial and tentative, having reference to the circumstances of a few places and of a particular time.

This inevitable vagueness is more felt by us, now that we have learnt to distinguish between traditional Christianity and the religion of Christ. As dogmatic theology relaxes its hold upon the mind, we become

aware of the continued need of some ideal support
for morality; and while we seek for this first and
chiefly in the New Testament, we also feel afresh the
undying value of other pages, 'rich with the spoils of
time,' which have preserved for us a different type of
excellence, not reaching, perhaps, to the celestial
heights, but looking down upon us from the calm
summits of human things.

The religious atmosphere in which many of us grew
up was full of the exaggerations of mediævalism—
exaggerations of sin, of holiness, of asceticism, of
chivalry, of the terrors of another world. How
far these may be traced to Scandinavian or Teutonic
antecedents, we need not stop to enquire. But a true
antidote for them is to be found in the Greek spirit, of
which the essence was a moderation by no means
inconsistent with the most burning enthusiasm.

This must at least be one chief tone in that 'bodi-
less harmony' (κόσμος τις ἀσώματος *Plato, Philebus*) to
which we look for assistance in the regulation of human
life, if the past is anything to us, and physical science
is not our all in all. But it must be remembered that
the best ideas of any age and country are, as it were,
encased in limitations, which they must transcend,
if they are to be made available in another time and
place. The highest thoughts of the Greeks have
come to us from the most aristocratic section of a
society that was based on slavery. But already in Plato

the nobler elements of Greek thought had burst the sheath of language, and the conceptions of nobleness, and of liberality, have fortunately still a meaning for us, though equality of rights has been asserted, and slavery is doomed; just as the more modern notion of 'courtesy' may, we hope, retain something of significance, even where the 'courts of princes, where it first was named,' have never existed, or have been swept away.

And this may be taken as a sample of the general truth, that whatsoever things are good and true should be fearlessly accepted and used, notwithstanding the very different elements which may have clung to them at the time and in the place of their birth.

ADDRESS.

On some Meeting Points between Christianity and Hellenic Culture.

In reading the Bible, or any great inspiring book, an enthusiastic fancy is apt to exclaim, 'Oh, to have lived in those days; to have heard such words from the lips of those who spoke them; to have witnessed these scenes ; perchance to have acted in them!' But if such thoughts ever cross our minds, there are second thoughts which tell us that 'we know not what we ask.' We see the far-off light, and are caught by its radiance, and we forget the barrenness and desolation from the midst

of which it shines.   What we really covet are not the
circumstances, but the spirit and the power to cope
with them, which even when thus surrounded could
so act and speak.   To live in the times of prophets
and apostles, we should have needed the strength
of a prophet or an apostle.   A moment's reflection
shows us that, being what we are, we cannot wish to
have been with Elijah on Mount Carmel, or with
St. Paul at Ephesus or at Cæsarea.

And even so it is when we meditate on that
Gentile world to which your thoughts are often
directed in this place.   From thence also there
comes to us a light and a voice which we cannot
dispense with, whose value is indefeasible and inexhaustible.   But the light comes from a place of tombs,
and the voice is that of a sybil in her cave.   No
rational man would restore the life of heathenism, if
he could ; and however much it were desired, it is
happily impossible.   It had its brighter and its
darker side, and so has our modern life ; but we would
not exchange our miseries for theirs.   What we do
desire is that we might enter into the fulness of our
inheritance, by making our own the thoughts, the
examples, the creations of former time, which are imperishable.   Like all high thoughts, all noble examples, and all fair creations, these rose far above the
level of contemporary life, and stood out in contrast,
and often in sharp antagonism, from the age which

gave them birth. If we labour to understand and represent to ourselves the details of that life, the characteristic features of that early time, it is only that we may more completely realize the grandeur and significance of those rare thoughts, examples, and imaginations.

When standing, as I did some months ago, on the Acropolis at Athens, and letting the eye range from the Areopagus in the foreground to the snowy ridge of Cyllene: or when feeling the flush of morning on the bay of Salamis, as the first rays darted from behind Pentelicus; or again, in climbing the island promontory, and surveying the shore of Attica from Eleusis to Peiræus—could we desire, even while enwrapt in the radiance of that magic light, that we ourselves were following some priest of Apollo up the ascent of the Propylæa ; or that the morning cloud we saw resting in the hollow beneath Eleusis, were in reality, as was once imagined, stirred up by the feet of the Mystæ, and that we ourselves were of them ? No man can for a moment wish to exchange a wider for a narrower horizon. Truly, if any age of the world could tempt us to wander back into it, the age of Æschylus and of Pericles would be that age. To have fought at Marathon, or to have seen the completion of the Parthenon, is a more enviable lot than to have been a courtier of King Solomon. But our own lot is far more enviable than either, if we only knew our advantages and how to use them. 'The heirs of all the ages,' no generation has been so rich in opportunities. The wisdom and the spiritual glories, not of one time and country only, whether of Solomon or of Solon, but of many eras and of many climes, the best thoughts, the noblest aspirations, the holiest counsels of the best, the holiest, the greatest human souls, are ours, if we will open our minds and hearts to them, not as dead tradition, but alive and potent to inspire and guide. The book of nature is unrolled for us more widely than ever before. And high above all, endued with sovereign alchemy to detect and purge the faults of human things, to reinforce whatever is pure and lovely and of good report, to take it up into the heavenly places and to redouble its value, we have the spirit of Christ; if, through our imperfection, less intensely realized by us than by the first Christians, yet perhaps seen more truly in its manifold relations to other more partial and limited expressions of what is highest in man.

This brings me to the point to which I would direct attention during the time allotted me, the relation of Christianity to so-called heathen wisdom. It is a subject which we cannot overlook, if we desire, as in this place we must desire, to reconcile the spirit of culture with religious feeling. The two have sometimes been mischievously opposed; at other times no less mischievously confounded. Early Christianity naturally shrank with horror from any contact with paganism. It lay too near to the reality of the Græco-Roman life to be able to separate between the good and the evil, especially because the evil had reached to such heights of abominable corruption, and even much that had been good and beautiful had become degraded so as to minister to the evil. Still there were elements of truth and good in Gentile thought, which from their affinity to Christian doctrine could not but blend with it, and indeed, even before Christ, had already met and mingled at Alexandria with Jewish tradition. Much that the example of Christ condemned had already been condemned in theory by Greek philosophers, who thus enforced intellectually the deeper spiritual influence : the Unseen Eternal God of the Jews was the goal toward which Greek thought had tended in its singular reaction from polytheism ; the Christian hope of resurrection bore a close relationship to the idea of immortality. Thus, even when most vehemently opposed to all that was of pagan origin, when separated by the deepest gulf from the heathen world, when hatred of idols and dæmons, and the sensuality which accompanied them, had been most intensified by persecution, exile, and poverty, the battle of the Christian believers was already waged in part with weapons taken from the armoury which the higher mind of heathenism had itself provided.

. . . . . .

Again, after many centuries in which Christianity had been, at least nominally, the religion of Europe, but in which Christian tradition, after leavening the world, had been not a little darkened and corrupted, the literature of antiquity reappeared as a new-found treasure. The immediate effect of this was by no means unmixed good. On the one hand, an heir-loom priceless in itself was secured for transmission to posterity, and an impulse was given to every form of intellectual energy, which is still felt to vibrate amidst the complex influences of to-day. But on the other hand, in the reaction from mediæval austerity, the principle of humanism, ' Homo sum, nihil humani a me alienum puto,' ' I am a man, and count nothing human alien to me,' received too indiscriminate and too superficial application, even to the partial oblitera-tion of some chief outlines of the Christian ideal. Christianity, having for a time missed something of human gentleness, was now destined to lose some-thing of religious purity. The touchstone which should have discerned the true gold from the dross, was either not there, or not carefully enough applied ; and, to speak roughly, Christendom has since oscil-lated between libertinism and Puritanism in various forms. Perhaps the contrast between the higher and the lower aspect of the Renaissance has nowhere been more finely touched than in a romance of our own day, the story of Romola, in which immediately after the death of Lorenzo the Magnificent, there comes upon the scene a plausible Greekling, of boundless versatility of talent, with great powers, but all of them superficial, and without a heart. I have often admired the artistic skill and the profound meaning of that introduction.

A different, and in some respects a higher mission than that of merely continuing either the Hebrew or the classical tradition, seems to devolve upon our age. The time seems to have come when we can in some measure distinguish what is highest and noblest in antiquity from that which is base or imperfect, that which is kindred or supplementary to Christianity from that which Christianity condemns. To speak for a moment in Scripture language, we may hope so to have learned Christ. that nothing in humanity can be harmful to us: because if good or innocent, it will mingle with the breathing of His spirit and be transfigured by it : if bad or mean, it will be judged and rejected by Him, and trodden under our feet. And the good which we so find may be of great value to us, even though, when we look again at the documents of our religion, we fancy that it might have been found there also from the first.

I know that there is another and, as some may think, a larger way of regarding this whole subject, according to which the antiquities of Greece and Rome are regarded as a moment in the development of human nature, and as one of many portions or samples of human experience. From this anthropological stand-point, Greek history is only more important than Mexican or Peruvian history, in that it is more fully recorded. This, however, is not the aspect of antiquity of which I am now speaking. What I desire to urge is that we should prize and make our own, in true conformity with the teaching of Christ, all that is highest and noblest in the thoughts, the imaginations, the active principles of some of the best and wisest of our race.

Let us premise that there are three cardinal points in which Greek wisdom comes far short of the humblest Christian teaching; namely, in its tolerance of sensuality, of cruelty, and of pride.

1. The first of these failings is perhaps the most conspicuous. Not that many ancients were not deeply impressed with the dignity and grace of purity. This could not be more finely felt by any one, than it is by Æschylus in his tragedies. But there was not one of their writers, however capable of moral sublimity, who in his lighter moods could not jest at things which, as we well know, are not matters for jesting but for abhorrence : not because we are better than they—very far from that—but because of two things coming between us and them, a good thing and an evil thing—the life of Christ,

seen first in the Gospels and since reflected in the lives of many Christians, and—twenty centuries of human misery. We know too well what have been the fountains that have chiefly fed that misery, whence flows the poison which the waters of Israel have not yet purged away, to dwell with a light heart, as they did, on the blots of that ancient life. And we have seen the image of One who condemns them, not with repulsive austerity, but through the beauty of holiness. We may admire their gaiety and freshness of temper, but we have felt too much to be either attracted or injured by their levity.

2. And then, to pass from this, we have heard words which make repulsive to us the cruelty and vindictiveness, which cling even to the most generous utterances of the ancient world. Although such sayings as these have not yet had their full effect, 'Whosoever shall offend one of these little ones;' 'Their angels do always behold the face of my Father who is in Heaven;' 'Inasmuch as ye have done it unto one of the least of these, ye have done it unto me;' yet they have sunk deep into the heart of Christendom, and have given rise to possibilities of feeling which the noblest hearts of ancient Hellas could not have conceived. And if the precept, 'Love your enemies,' has not yet tamed the passions of men; yet in this and that other precept, 'Whatsoever ye would that men should do to you, do ye even so to them.' a standard

has been lifted which has permanently raised the level of our moral judgments. I cannot admit that even the great precept, ' Do not to another what you would not that another should do to you,' comes nearly to the height of the Christian golden rule. The one is negative and limited ; the other is positive and inexhaustible. The one teaches me not to offend my neighbour ; the other urges me to do everything I possibly can to benefit him. It is interesting to note where, in this respect, great minds in earlier times have approached the Christian standard. But we must acknowledge that they came far short of it. I may just hint at the contrast that might be drawn between the treatment of his sons by Œdipus in the ancient poem of atonement, and the treatment of his enemies by Prospero.

3. Again, the ancient ideal of virtue was hardly separable from pride and contempt for others. Christianity, by presenting a type of perfection before which all feel their sinfulness, and also by revealing the value of each individual soul before God, has given a new meaning and importance to the grace of humility.

But there are other lessons which Christian teaching has not always supplied with equal clearness, and which are brought home to us in the reading of Greek literature. I will mention a few of these.

And it may sound strangely to you if I give the

first place to the love of home. We are apt to think of this as an especially Christian virtue. But the circumstances of the first Christians, in which a man's foes were they of his own household, the exaggerations of asceticism, and consequent misapplication of the words, ' He that loveth father or mother more than me, is unworthy of me,' have sometimes been anything but favourable to domestic life. It is true that Greek home life was not like ours. But their defects in this respect make all the more striking the lessons which are taught in their poetry. Where else will you find such tremendous sanctions assigned to domestic virtue, as understood by them ; where else more fascinating pictures of the attachment of children to a father, of brother to sister, and sister to brother, of mother to child, aye even of wife to husband ? One of the most obvious characteristics of Greek poetry is the close juxtaposition of extreme tenderness and extreme vindictiveness. The tenderness and the vindictiveness spring ofttimes from the same root, the sanctity of the domestic hearth. I have not time to quote examples, but I will refer to one, the same on which Dr. Arnold used to dwell so often, the last parting of the old Theban outcast from his daughters, where he reminds them of the abundant affection which had softened all the hardships they had borne for him.

The instances of true tenderness, of exquisite pathos,

of faithful and pure feeling, from the lament of Briseis
over Hector downwards, cannot be numbered. If the
New Testament sets before us a divine ideal, which
satisfies our highest aspirations and corrects our
faults; yet there are also deep veins of human
emotion, having a peculiar sacredness, which find a
clearer and fuller and more varied expression in what
has been called profane literature. And just as there
are moods, in which we find more comfort in some
parts of the Old Testament than in the New; so
there are true and noble feelings of the heart, which
find a response in Greek poetry which does not
equally come to us from the Bible.

One of these feelings is the reverence for human
law, which was more reconcilable than we are apt to
suppose with the love of liberty and the hatred of
tyranny. It is in the same sentence, that Pericles
boasts of the freedom of private life at Athens, and in
which he says, 'We respect the authority of the
magistrate and of the laws, especially those of them
which are unwritten, and are made for the defence of
the oppressed.' Christianity is of course in a still higher
sense the obedience to an unwritten law, to a spiritual
principle written on the tablet of the heart. But
coming from a country that was doomed, and from
a nation that rejected it, the earliest Christianity could
not give that direct sanction to the love of country,
and to national piety, which lay so deep in the better

spirits of Greece. The lament of St. Paul over his countrymen, of Christ over Jerusalem, show that this also was of the essence of the new religion. But not till it had bound all nations into one could it be clearly seen how profoundly in harmony with the love of country, as well as of kindred, was the worship which in its first origin 'brought not peace, but a sword.' To the best minds of Greece, the love of civic order and the love of liberty were one. For by liberty they meant nothing else but the continuance of that order to which their hearts gave loyal and willing obedience, because it came to them from their sires, and was sanctioned by all that they esteemed as holy in their land.

Let us name another characteristic of the best Greek literature, in which I think that it contrasts favourably with the literature of the nations which have professed Christianity. This is, in one word, its manliness. In modern countries, I know not for what reason, the literary spirit has often been strangely allied to softness and effeminacy. The best Greek poetry is pre-eminently masculine. I do not speak of the Æolian lyric poetry, or of the poetry of the declining period, which has a special charm of its own, but of the main stream of the earlier poetry. In point of wholesomeness and strength, to leave other qualities for the present out of view, what modern poet, perhaps excepting Dante, can be com-

pared to Homer, or to Æschylus, or Pindar? We
are somewhat apt to be imposed upon by the form
of contrast, and especially perhaps by the contrast
between things spiritual and things secular. And
I cannot but think that there is something of logical
illusion in the opposition so often made between
Hebraism and Hellenism, as if these were two principles mutually exclusive of each other. Else I
think we should have acknowledged more fully than
has yet been done, the increasing moral purpose
running through Greek literature, and constituting a
revelation of righteousness, which if less imperious, is
hardly less persuasive than in the prophetic writings.
It is true that the ideas of justice and of vengeance
cling together, and are but slowly and imperfectly
separated. But is not this equally the case in the
Old Testament? And can we altogether spare the
sterner aspects of justice, which were more natural
to the ancient world? But for a habit of language,
which on the whole it is wiser to observe, would
there be any impropriety in speaking of the progressive utterance of this idea as a revelation?

First comes the hint of powers that chasten the
perjured after death, which strikes us by its isolated
solemnity in Homer; then the Nemesis, though
darkened with envy, that so profoundly impressed
Herodotus as coming from God; then the higher conception of a supreme deity, combining righteousness,

wisdom, and faithfulness, with almighty strength, that mingles like a tone of genuine Hebraic melody with the clear Hellenic harmonies of Æschylus; then the crystalline empyrean, where the unwritten law of piety and mercy is enthroned above the Muse of Sophocles; and lastly, the ideal righteous man of Plato, who cannot harm even an enemy, but like the divinity of whose nature he partakes, can only be the cause of good.   Whether we regard all this as a conscious preparation for the Gospel, or as a lower stage of revelation, or as a confirmation of revelation through the law written on the Gentile heart and mind, we cannot dispense with the instruction which it still holds forth to us, at a time when 'victorious analysis,' if I may borrow a happy phrase, is threatening even the foundations of morality.

I have tried to dwell on some of the less obvious aspects of the subtle and manifold influence of Greek literature.   That it ministers, as no sacred books can do, to the intellectual virtues, and to these moral virtues that are most allied to them, 'Self-reverence, self-knowledge, self-control,'—that it gives us an ideal of equal friendship almost unrivalled; that it refines æsthetic perceptions; that without it the love of knowledge and of truth is apt to pine and wither— it hardly needs to say.   What science, and ethical reflection, and the fine arts owe to Greece is a common theme.   It can hardly be necessary to urge that the study of Greek books should be carefully directed to ends which they are known to serve so well.

But I may conclude with one general observation. Except in its first sacred outgoings, our religion has been always liable to the dangers of narrowness and extravagance. In Greek literature we have a spirit of moderation that is not inconsistent with the highest aspiration and enthusiasm. That practical wisdom which is skilful in the choice of means, that clear insight without which the highest impulses are doomed to frustration, that conscious study of human nature so indispensable for all who would teach or guide mankind—have all their most fruitful exemplars in Greek culture.

The more comprehensively we learn to view the world of man and nature, and the more firmly we have learned to hold the essential principles of the Christian life, the less we shall feel able to forego our communion with those few great souls, who soar like eagles above the clouds of time, and whose utterances, to adapt a saying of Heraclitus, penetrate to far more than a thousand years.

Salvation Here and Hereafter. Sermons and Essays by the Rev. JOHN SERVICE, Minister of Inch. New Edition. Crown 8vo., 6s.

Through Nature to Christ : or, The Ascent of Worship through Illusion to the Truth. By the Rev. E. A. ABBOTT, D.D., Head Master of the City of London School. 8vo., 12s. 6d.

The Difficulties of Belief in connection with the Creation and Fall, Redemption, and Judgment. By the Rev. Prof. BIRKS. Second Edition, Enlarged. Crown 8vo., 5s.

The Apostolical Fathers : a Critical Account of their Genuine Writings and of their Doctrines. By JAMES DONALDSON, LL.D. Crown 8vo., 7s. 6d.

Ecce Homo. A Survey of the Life and Work of Jesus Christ. Eleventh Edition. Crown 8vo., 6s.

The Victory of Faith. By JULIUS CHARLES HARE, M.A., Archdeacon of Lewes. Edited by Professor PLUMPTRE. With Introductory Notices by the late Professor MAURICE and Dean STANLEY. Third Edition. Crown 8vo., 6s. 6d.

The Mission of the Comforter. By the late Archdeacon HARE. Edited with Notes by Professor E. H. PLUMPTRE. New Edition. Crown 8vo., 7s. 6d.

By John M'Leod Campbell, D.D.

The Nature of the Atonement, and its Relation to Remission of Sins and Eternal Life. Fourth Edition. Crown 8vo., 6s.

Christ the Bread of Life. Second Edition, greatly enlarged. Crown 8vo., 4s. 6d.

Reminiscences and Reflections, referring to his Early Ministry in the Parish of Row, 1825-31. Edited with an Introductory Narrative by his son, DONALD CAMPBELL, M.A. Crown 8vo., 7s. 6d.

Thoughts on Revelation. with special reference to the Present Time. Second Edition. Crown 8vo., 5s.

MACMILLAN & CO., LONDON.

By the late Canon Kingsley.

The Water of Life, and other Sermons. Second Edition. Fcap. 8vo., 3s. 6d.

The Gospel of the Pentateuch. Second Edition. 3s. 6d.

Good News of God. Sixth Edition. Crown 8vo., 6s.

Sermons for the Times. Third Edition. 3s. 6d.

Village, Town and Country Sermons. New Edition. Crown 8vo., 6s.

Sermons on National Subjects. Second Edition. 3s. 6d.

The King of the Earth, and other Sermons. Second Edition. Fcap. 8vo., 3s. 6d.

Discipline, and other Sermons. Fcap. 8vo., 3s. 6d.

David. Five Sermons. Second Edition, Enlarged. 2s. 6d.

Westminster Sermons. 8vo., 10s. 6d.

By Canon Farrar, D.D., F.R.S.

In the Days of thy Youth. Sermons on Practical Subjects preached at Marlborough College, 1871–1876. Third Edition. Crown 8vo., 9s.

The Fall of Man; and other Sermons. Third Edition. 6s.

The Witness of History to Christ; being the Hulsean Lectures for 1870. Fourth Edition. Crown 8vo., 5s.

Seekers after God. The Lives of Seneca, Epictetus, and Marcus Aurelius. New Edition. Crown 8vo., 6s.

The Silence and Voices of God. University and other Sermons. Third Edition. Crown 8vo., 6s.

By Canon Westcott, D.D.

A General Survey of the History of the Canon of the New Testament during the First Four Centuries. Third Edition, Revised. Crown 8vo., 10s. 6d.

Introduction to the Study of the Gospels. Fifth Edition. Crown 8vo., 10s. 6d.

The Bible in the Church. A Popular Account of the Collection and Reception of the Holy Scriptures in the Christian Churches. New Edition. 18mo., 4s. 6d.

MACMILLAN & CO., LONDON.

www.ingramcontent.com/pod-product-compliance
Lightning Source LLC
Chambersburg PA
CBHW030629030726
47497CB00006B/1696